AF400656

The Language of Literacy Education

The Language of Education

Key Terms and Concepts in Teaching and Learning

Series Editor

William F. McComas (*Parks Family Distinguished Professor of Science Education, University of Arkansas, Fayetteville, AR, USA*)

VOLUME 2

The titles published in this series are listed at *brill.com/tloe*

The Language of Literacy Education

Edited by

Vicki Stewart Collet

BRILL

LEIDEN | BOSTON

All chapters in this book have undergone peer review.

The Library of Congress Cataloging-in-Publication Data is available online at http://catalog.loc.gov

Typeface for the Latin, Greek, and Cyrillic scripts: "Brill". See and download: brill.com/brill-typeface.

ISSN 2666-0121
ISBN 978-90-04-50325-0 (paperback)
ISBN 978-90-04-50326-7 (hardback)
ISBN 978-90-04-50339-7 (e-book)

Contents

Preface and Introduction

Literacy education is circuitously word-focused. To teach about words, we must know about words. More expansively, researching, teaching, and leading in the field of literacy education requires understanding of how specific words are applied within the field. Refining that understanding is the goal of this volume.

Words are *representational*; they represent things and ideas. They stand for, depict, and signify these things and ideas. They are used to say something meaningful about the world to other people. Words are an essential part of how meaning is created and exchanged (Hall, 1997). Precision in their use, therefore, enhances the creation and exchange of meaning.

Words are also *constitutive*; they make things (Johnston, 2004). Words build ideas and identities, roles, and realities. They position people. They bring things into existence. As we ponder ideas, we work our way through them with words, and we find words to express them. "Language is the dress of thought" (Johnson, in Ratcliff, 2017). Language is wrapped around ideas to give them form and function.

In Shakespeare's famous play, Juliet states: "What's in a name? That which you call a rose by any other name would smell as sweet" (Romeo and Juliet, Act II, Scene II). But research does not seem to bear out Juliet's hope. The words that are available to you influence what you perceive. For example, the Inuit have over 100 words for snow, and they recognize all of the differences these terms connote. Language actually influences our perceptual systems (Harre & Gillet, 1994). It affects what you notice and learn. To this end, we offer a list of terms to guide our noticing and learning.

In this volume, we seek to represent the language of literacy education. However, in doing so, we, the authors, acknowledge that we have constructed our own meaning of this language. Because language is constitutive, its meaning is not final or fixed (Bakhtin, 1981). Word meanings change over time and across contexts. Even when meanings seem static, connotations, the ideas or feelings that a word invokes, shift. As a tool for constructing meaning, language is not fixed, but fluid. Because of this flexibility and fluidity, there is no final word about the language of literacy education. Acknowledging this reality, we recognize that an objective definition of terms is impossible. The descriptions in this volume represent expansive sampling of the literature in the field, interpreted through the experience of the authors. We position ourselves as ongoing learners of the language of literacy education.

We hope that, by giving descriptions of terms, we provide a tool for reading, writing, and thinking about literacy education. Language has been described as the "tool of tools" (Dewey, 1958, p. 58). Language facilitates communication; the language of literacy education allows researchers, teachers, and other literacy leaders to exchange ideas, communicating with precision. Language plays an important function as a tool for learning.

Organization of This Volume

The 87 main entries in this volume are organized alphabetically, listed in the Table of Contents, and italicized and bolded when included in another entry. However, additional important terms are included within each entry; these are italicized, and you will find them in the index. Consulting the index will lead to a term's relations with a variety of topics, and perusing these will allow readers to construct their own meaning. Where two or more of the main entries are closely related, you will find a bracketed "See also" notation at the end of the entry. Also bracketed at the end of the entry is the name of the author who contributed the term. Together, the thirteen authors of this book represent a range of knowledge about literacy learning, with expertise about literacy learning from birth to university and beyond. Sociocultural, constructivist, cognitive, and critical *perspectives* are represented. As editor, I am indebted to my co-authors for their expansive knowledge, their insight, and their keen attention to detail. I believe their work here clarifies the language of literacy education.

Acknowledgments

In addition to acknowledging the excellent work of this volume's contributors, I want to especially thank Dr. William McComas for extending to us the opportunity to contribute to the "Language of Education" series. When approached by Bill, my colleague in the Department of Curriculum and Instruction at the University of Arkansas, I immediately recognized the value that the *Language of Literacy Education* could make to the profession. What surprised me (and this has been echoed by co-authors) was how much I learned through writing about terms that I, purportedly, already knew. Examining the wide ways that the terms have been and are being used in the field has proved a productive experience. I'm thus indebted to Dr. McComas for deepening my own understanding of the language of literacy education. Finally, the authors are appreciative of our anonymous reviewer, whose insightful and detailed feedback has significantly strengthened our work.

Note

The main entries were selected for inclusion in this volume through a survey of scholars in the field. We acknowledge the plethora of terms that could have been included and recognize that some significant terms have likely been omitted. We welcome the feedback of the reader for terms that might be considered for subsequent editions. Additionally, in recognizing that use of the terms we have included is fluid, we welcome feedback on our representation of terms. Evolving definitions of the language of literacy education will offer "ever new ways to mean" (Bakhtin, 1981, p. 346).

Bakhtin, M. M. (1981). *The dialogic imagination* (M. Holquist & C. Emerson, Trans. and Ed.). University of Austin Press.

Dewey, J. (1958). *Experience and nature*. Dover Publications, Inc.

Hall, S. (1997). Representation, meaning and language. In S. Hall (Ed.), *Representation: Cultural representations and signifying practices* (pp. 15–64). Sage.

Harre, R., & Gillet, G. (1994). *The discursive mind*. Sage.

Johnston, P. H. (2004). *Choice words: How our language affects children's learning*. Stenhouse Publishers.

Ratcliffe, S. (Ed.). (2017). *Oxford essential quotations* (6th ed.). Oxford University Press. https://www.oxfordreference.com/view/10.1093/acref/9780191843730.001.0001/q-oro-ed5-00005955

Notes on Contributors

Johnny B. Allred
earned a Ph.D. in 2020 from the University of Arkansas and is a visiting assistant professor in the English Department at Brigham Young University. His research centers on English education and technology integration in literacy instruction.

Rebecca Carpenter de Cortina
is a research associate at the University of Arkansas. Her areas of interest include languaging, bilingual education, and family engagement. Rebecca holds a master's in international educational development from Teachers College and is currently pursuing a doctorate in Curriculum & Instruction.

Leah R. Cheek
has served as a teacher, laboratory preschool director, and adjunct professor. She is co-author of *STEM Integration through 3D-Printing and Modeling* and a Doctoral Academy Fellow Ph.D. Candidate in Curriculum and Instruction at the University of Arkansas.

Vicki Stewart Collet
is associate professor of curriculum and instruction at the University of Arkansas. She received a Ph.D. in Reading Education from the University at Buffalo in 2011. She is author of *Collaborative Lesson Study: ReVisioning Teacher Professional Development*.

Judy L. Fields
is a literacy specialist for Northwest Arkansas Education Service Cooperative. Her primary interest is reading comprehension. Judy holds a specialist's degree from Henderson State University and is completing doctoral studies in curriculum and instruction at University of Arkansas.

Seth D. French
teaches secondary English and Media Literacy at Bentonville High School (Arkansas). Noted as a "30 Under 30" awardee in 2021 by the International Literacy Association, Seth earned his Ph.D. from the University of Arkansas in July 2020.

Savanna L. Gragg

is a graduate assistant at the University of Arkansas and a doctoral candidate focusing on early childhood professional learning. Savanna coauthored *The Impact of a Relationship-Building Strategy on Teachers' Perceptions of Preschooler Behavior: A 2 × 10 Approach* with Vicki Collet.

Angelia C. Greiner

is a literacy specialist for the Northwest Arkansas Educational Service Center. Her areas of interest including writing instruction and culturally responsive pedagogy. She has a Ph.D. in Curriculum & Instruction from the University of Arkansas.

Megan Yates Grizzle

has taught secondary English students for the past nine years. She is currently pursuing a Ph.D. in Curriculum and Instruction at the University of Arkansas-Fayetteville where she received a Doctoral Academy Fellowship.

Kathryn Hackett-Hill

is a doctoral student at the University of Arkansas. A National Writing Project Teacher-Consultant and ARTeacher Fellow, she recently published an article in *English Journal.*

Holly Sheppard Riesco

is a former ELA teacher and a doctoral student in Curriculum and Instruction in English Education at the University of Arkansas. She is the co-author of *Adolescent Realities: Engaging Students in SEL through Young Adult Literature.*

Afton Schleiff

received her specialist degree in Educational Leadership from Arkansas State University. She has a bachelor's degree in English and a master's degree in Teaching from the University of Arkansas. Currently, she works as an Instructional Facilitator in Springdale, Arkansas.

Wyann Stanton

(M.Ed.) has a passion and talent for teaching students and teachers along the continuum of learning. Wyann earned her Ph.D. from the University of Arkansas in July 2021.

Annotation is the process in which readers study and respond to texts by highlighting passages, writing in the margins, or otherwise adding to or amending the original text with their thoughts. Research shows that annotation, whether paper-based or online, improves reading outcomes because it requires students to actively construct ideas and monitor their learning as they read (Porter-O'Donnell, 2004; Simpson & Nist, 1990).

Kalir and Garcia (2019) highlight five main purposes for annotation: (a) to share information, making knowledge more accessible; (b) to provide commentary, making *perspectives* more transparent; (c) to express power, challenging traditional authorities; (d) to stimulate conversation, making reading more dialogic; and to aid in *understanding,* enhancing what is learned from texts. Simpson and Nist (1990) suggest that, in classroom settings, students should be taught explicitly how to annotate, including such steps as previewing the text, reading carefully, stopping to think, paraphrasing key ideas, and reflecting on their annotations after reading. While reading literary texts, students can create annotation categories to organize their thoughts about *characters, setting, vocabulary, plot elements,* and the writer's craft (Porter-O'Donnell, 2004).

Digital technology has brought about the possibility of *online annotation*—annotation on digital platforms with web capability—enabling readers to annotate web articles, e-books, YouTube videos, or other digital texts. Moving annotation online also allows readers to engage in *social annotation,* where they can see others' comments on the texts they are reading and engage in dialogue that is not limited by time or physical space (Glover, Xu, & Hardaker, 2007). In the classroom, *literacy* teachers can use online annotation with apps such as Hypothesis as a platform for their students—whether in or out of the classroom—to discuss the texts they are reading, thereby supporting their *comprehension* and preparing them for follow-up activities and extension (Allred, 2020). [Contributed by Johnny B. Allred]

Allred, J. B. (2020). *Web annotation in English language arts: Online dialogue as a platform to support student comprehension of texts* [Doctoral dissertation]. University of Arkansas. ProQuest (Publication No. 27995957).

Glover, I., Xu, Z., & Hardaker, G. (2007). Online annotation: Research and practices. *Computers & Education, 49*(4), 1308–1320.

Kalir, J. H., & Garcia, A. (2019). *Annotation.* MIT Press.

Porter-O'Donnell, C. (2004). Beyond the yellow highlighter: Teaching annotation skills to improve reading comprehension. *The English Journal, 93*(5), 82–89.

Simpson, M. L., & Nist, S. L. (1990). Textbook annotation: An effective and efficient study strategy for college students. *Journal of Reading, 34*(2), 122–129.

Argumentative writing is a *genre* of writing that includes the construction of *claims, evidence, warrants, backing*, and *rebuttals* to make logical appeals to the reader (Hillocks, 2011). Distinct from *opinion writing* or *persuasive writing*—which emphasize emotional appeals and the use of rhetoric to persuade—argumentative writing, when done effectively, includes reasoning and evidence from multiple sources that advance written claims in logical and valid ways (Hillocks, 2011).

Newell, VanDerHeide, and Wynhoff Olsen (2014) suggest that, while argumentative writing in the classroom is often oversimplified and overly prescribed (e.g., teachers giving students preset forms for argumentative essays), *literacy* educators should broaden their vision of argumentative writing to more fully consider the complexities of argumentation, such as the need to balance form and content, or the **understanding** of how to write argumentatively for a variety of *audiences* and in a variety of *contexts*. Ferretti and Lewis (2013) propose two instructional strategies for meaningful argumentative writing in the classroom: teachers should incorporate writing activities that have real audiences, and they should allow students some *choice* in selecting a topic that they genuinely care about. These approaches will *motivate* students to identify and organize appropriate evidence and include sound reasoning to support the claims they make in their writing.

In our digital world, where virtually anybody can share their arguments with a global audience, literacy educators are tasked with teaching about the dangers of *propaganda*, or the sharing of ideas—typically biased or misleading ideas—designed to change the behavior or beliefs of a group of people. Hobbs and McGee (2014) assert that *critical thinking*, the type of thinking that should pervade argumentative writing in literacy settings, is developed as students engage with others' **perspectives** and claims in order to shape and strengthen their own arguments and understandings of the world. [Contributed by Johnny B. Allred] [See also Thesis]

Ferretti, R. P., & Lewis, W. E. (2013). Best practices in teaching argumentative writing. In S. Graham, C.A. MacArthur, & J. Fitzgerald (Eds.), *Best practices in writing instruction* (2nd ed., pp. 113–140). Guilford.

Hillocks, G. H. (2011). *Teaching argument writing, grades 6–12: Supporting claims with relevant evidence and clear reasoning.* Heinemann.

Hobbs, R., & McGee, S. (2014). Teaching about propaganda: An examination of the historical roots of media literacy. *Journal of Media Literacy Education, 6*(2), 56–57.

Newell, G. E., VanDerHeide, J., & Wynhoff Olsen, A. (2014). High school English language arts teachers' argumentative epistemologies for teaching writing. *Research in the Teaching of English, 49*(2), 95–119.

Assessment provides instructors with information regarding learner performance and may be divided into two categories: formal assessment and informal assessment (Garcia & Pearson, 1991). *Formal assessment* is often associated with *standardized tests* which are summative in nature and designed to assess learner performance based on a predetermined set of criteria (Garcia & Pearson). Such assessments are referred to as *criterion-referenced assessments*. Formal assessments may also be *norm-referenced assessments*, which compare a learner's performance to other learners in a testing group.

Criterion-referenced assessments measure progress toward a criterion and may be ranked by performance levels such as exceeding, proficient, basic, or below basic. Norm-referenced tests usually report percentile ranking based on a bell curve. Both types of assessment are often associated with high-stakes tests administered one time per year for accountability and are summative in nature. Formal assessments may also include summative assessments that measure student performance based on a unit of study. Such assessments may be textbook or program-specific measures that place students in a variety of levels for instruction (Garcia & Pearson, 1991).

Other types of **literacy assessment** can be categorized as either formative or informal assessment (Dann, 2019) and may include informal reading inventories (IRI), descriptive rubrics, portfolios, anecdotal records, teacher-made tests, *progress monitoring*, self-assessment, and teacher feedback. Descriptive *rubrics* are often based on a scale of performance to represent student achievement. *Informal reading inventories* measure reading progress and developmental approximations. *Portfolios* are a compilation of student work and include student reflection (Garcia & Pearson, 1991). *Anecdotal records,* such as **miscue analysis** (Goodman, 1996) and **running records,** are used to assess student performance during oral reading (Harmey & Kabuto, 2018). Thoughtful teacher feedback, especially from informal assessments, can support students' self-efficacy through the building of positive relationships (Dann, 2019). [Contributed by Judy L. Fields]

Dann, R. (2019). Feedback as a relational concept in the classroom. *The Curriculum Journal,* *30*(4), 352–374.

Garcia, G. E., & Pearson, P. D. (1991). *Literacy assessment in a diverse society.* Center for the Study of Reading Technical Report, No. 525.

Goodman, Y. M. (1996). Revaluing readers while readers revalue themselves: Retrospective miscue analysis. *The Reading Teacher, 49*(8), 600–609.

Harmey, S., & Kabuto, B. (2018). Metatheoretical differences between running records and miscue analysis: Implications for analysis of oral reading behaviors. *Research in the Teaching of English, 53*(1), 11–33.

Background knowledge, or *prior knowledge*, stems from previous experiences, interactions, social roles, institutions, cultures, and ideas (Anderson, 2019; Hatton & Lupo, 2020). Background knowledge is what is known about a topic or concept and is activated through *schemata*, the categorizations or connections that allow for assimilation of knowledge when encountering a new concept (Anderson, 2019). Background knowledge influences the focus and takeaways that students develop during a lesson.

For instructional purposes, teachers may assess background knowledge before introducing a concept. Anticipation guides (Fisher et al., 2016) or KWL charts (Hatton & Lupo, 2020) are common background knowledge strategies that aid in developing lessons to meet students' academic needs. By assessing what students already know, teachers can connect new knowledge to students' prior experiences to create purposeful ***understanding*** of concepts. Further, revisiting anticipation guides or KWL charts when a unit ends reinforces student metacognitive awareness of learning (Fisher et al., 2016).

Background knowledge may include misunderstandings and foster negligible connections that do not enhance learning (Harvey & Goudvis, 2007). In assessing prior knowledge, instructors also seek the misconceptions and shallow knowledge that negatively affects learning (Fisher et al., 2016). Extending background knowledge while developing awareness of misunderstandings allows students to rearrange erroneous background knowledge that lacks a nuanced, *multi-**perspective*** view of concepts.

Teachers should also assess students' *funds of knowledge* and funds of *identity* (Gonzalez et al., 2004; Esteban-Guitart & Moll, 2014) that mediate students' experiences prior to, in, and out of the classroom. Adhering to disciplinary schema limits students' extension of knowledge and creates *inequities* in learning (Hatton & Lupo, 2020). Therefore, teachers who assess background knowledge should support and extend multicultural *perspectives*, experiences, and identities. [Contributed by Holly Sheppard Riesco]

Anderson, R. C. (1984). Learning to read in American schools. In R. C. Anderson, J. Osborn, & R. J. Tierney (Eds.), *Learning to read in American schools* (pp. 243–257). Erlbaum.

Esteban-Guitart, M., & Moll, L. C. (2014). Funds of identity: A new concept based on the funds of knowledge approach. *Culture and Psychology, 20*(1), 31–48.

Fisher, D., Frey, N., & Hattie, J. (2016). *Visible learning for literacy*. Corwin.

Gonzalez, N., Moll, L. C., & Amanti, C. (2004). *Funds of knowledge: Theorizing practices in households, communities, and classrooms*. Lawrence Erlbaum Associates.

Harvey, S., & Goudvis, A. (2007). *Strategies that work: Teaching comprehension for understanding and engagement* (2nd ed.). Stenhouse.

Hattan, C., & Lupo, S. M. (2020). Rethinking the role of knowledge in the literacy classroom. *Reading Research Quarterly, 55*(S1), S283–S298.

Biliteracy was initially defined as the ability to read and write in two languages (Goodman et al., 1979). Since then, as we continue reflect on our ever-changing world and ***understandings*** of language and ***literacy***, its core essence has inevitably evolved. Through Hornberger's original and revisited continua model, biliteracy was reconceptualized as "any and all instances in which communication occurs in two (or more) languages in or around writing" (Hornberger & Skilton-Sylvester, 2000, p. 96). Building on this ecological framework, others now describe biliteracy as a dynamic, complex process which draws on multiple platforms, integrated language systems, and lived experiences to actively engage in reading, writing, speaking, and thinking multiple languages in a continuous way (Hopewell & Escamilla, 2014; Reyes, 2006).

Biliteracy theories of acquisition and pedagogical approaches have also shifted (García & Kleifgen, 2020). If a more integrated approach is taken, then learners are called upon to apply their entire language repertoire to intertwine and build on concepts in a variety of social and cultural ***contexts*** (García & Kleifgen, 2020). In any case, learners must be empowered to help create spaces that embrace and leverage all of their language and literacy practices; teachers must support their students' linguistic features through an *assets-based approach* that centers around their multifaceted *identities* and lived experiences; and parents must encourage their children to read books, analyze *environmental print*, write letters, play games, or simply just talk about everyday concepts in both (or more) languages.

When promoting biliteracy, it is critical to emphasize that it is a complex, dynamic process that involves recognizing, discerning, and communicating in multiple ways, in various contexts, at any given moment time. Embracing biliteracy in this manner will not only create new **perspectives** on languaging and living, but will also foster a *community of learners* who create *collaborative* partnerships, celebrate *diversity*, and advocate *equitable opportunities* for all. [Contributed by Rebecca Carpenter de Cortina]

García, O., & Kleifgen, J. A. (2020). Translanguaging and literacies. *Reading Research Quarterly*, 55(4), 553–571.

Goodman, Y. M., Flores, B., & Goodman, K. S. (1979). *Reading in the bilingual classroom: Literacy and biliteracy*. National Clearinghouse for Bilingual Education.

Hopewell, S., & Escamilla, K. (2014). Biliteracy development in immersion contexts. *Journal of Immersion and Content-based Language Education*, 2(2), 181–195.

Hornberger, N. H., & Skilton-Sylvester, E. (2000). Revisiting the continua of biliteracy: International and critical perspectives. *Language and Education*, 14(2), 96–122.

Reyes, I. (2006). Exploring connections between emergent biliteracy and bilingualism. *Journal of Early Childhood Literacy*, 6(3), 267–292.

Close reading is an attentive investigation of a text in which a reader observes, interrogates, and analyzes various aspects of the text such as word choice, punctuation, or other elements of craft to interpret and create meaning. To close read is to be a responsible and responsive reader, one who recognizes that "writing is an intentional act" and who is therefore "alert to the intentions of the writer" (Newkirk, 2012, p. 95). Newkirk also envisions close reading as a form of "slow reading" in which readers "pause to reflect or reread or just savor the moment" (p. 3). Close reading, then, is the antithesis of unaware consumption; of distracted, disinterested reading; of a quick extraction of information from a text without careful attention and thought.

Fisher and Frey (2014) identify several key features commonly implemented in close reading instructional exercises: short, complex passages that range from three paragraphs to three pages; *repeated reading*; **annotation**; *text-dependent questions*; and **discussions** of the text using *academic language* and *argumentation*.

But close reading activities can be misused or overused. If such activities disconnect readers from texts by largely ignoring **readers' background knowledge** and reactions to the text, then readers can become passive and disengaged. Likewise, as Atwell (2007) argues, sometimes close reading strategies imposed by outside directives can severely disrupt a reader who is in the zone, unsettling the natural ebb—moments of reflecting on reading—and flow—moments of fully immersed, non-interrupted reading.

Therefore, close reading should be coupled with other components of reading development like **independent reading,** teacher **modeling,** and interactive *read-alouds* to establish robust reading curricula (Fisher & Frey, 2012). Additionally, Sullivan advocates for "'deep reading'—a process of inquiry built around 'challenging questions' and 'troublesome knowledge' as well as caution, humility, and open-mindedness" to help students become stronger readers and writers (2017, p. XXII). [Contributed by Kathryn Hackett-Hill]

Atwell, N. (2007). *The reading zone: How to help kids become skilled, passionate, habitual, critical readers.* Scholastic.

Fisher, D., & Frey, N. (2012). Close reading in elementary schools. *The Reading Teacher 66*(3), 179–188.

Fisher, D., & Frey, N. (2014). Close reading as an intervention for struggling middle school readers. *Journal of Adolescent & Adult Literacy, 57*(5), 367–376.

Newkirk, T. (2012). *The art of slow reading: Six time-honored practices for engagement.* Heinemann.

Sullivan, P., Tinberg, H., & Blau, S. (Eds.). (2017). *Deep reading: Teaching reading in the writing classroom.* National Council of Teachers of English.

Comprehension, as applied to written language, is a literal and inferential metacognitive process whereby meaning is derived from text. Comprehension occurs through accurate retrieval of suprasegmental and segmental aspects of language (Chan & Wade-Woolley, 2018). Comprehension is bolstered by the application of requisite skills such as *rhetorical, syntactical, morphological, **phonological,** and orthographic knowledge* (Van Merriënboer & Kirschner, 2017). Inclusively, comprehension involves "…three elements: the reader, the text, and the activity all embedded within the larger sociocultural *context* of reading" (Compton & Pearson, 2016, p. 223). Comprehension may also be influenced by *multimodal* representations of ideas as found in visual, aural, and procedural rhetoric as well as orality (Gee, 2015).

Literal comprehension is represented by recall of concrete facts exhibited through *retelling* and/or response to specific questions or prompts that elicit factual regurgitation or logical connections of explicit information within the text (Compton & Pearson, 2016; Duke, Pearson, Strachan, & Billman, 2011). For example, identification of a word's denotative meaning, a text's structure and a *summary* of a text may represent literal comprehension.

Inferential comprehension occurs when meaning is represented through interpretation involving **background knowledge** situated in cultural, linguistic, and academic experience (Duke et al., 2011). For example, inferential comprehension is displayed through identification and explanation of implicit symbolic features, abstraction, thematic implications, figurative language, ambiguity, and nuances of language such as *tone*, mood, and connotation of words and phrases. [Contributed by Judy L. Fields]

Chan, J. S., & Wade-Woolley L. (2018). Explaining phonology and reading in adult learners: Introducing prosodic awareness and executive function to reading ability. *Journal of Research in Reading*, 41(1), 42–57.

Compton, D.L., & Pearson, P.D. (2016). Identifying robust variation associated with reading comprehension skill: The search for pressure points. *Journal of Research on Educational Effectiveness*, 9(2), 223–231.

Duke, N. K., Pearson, P. D., Strachan, S. L., & Billman, A. K. (2011). Essential elements of fostering and teaching reading comprehension. In S. J. Samuels & A. E. Farstrup (Eds.), *What research has to say about reading instruction* (4th ed., pp. 51–93). International Reading Association.

Gee, J. P. (2015). *Social linguistics and literacies: Ideology in discourses*. Routledge.

Van Merriënboer, J. J., & Kirschner, P. A. (2017). *Ten steps to complex learning: A systematic approach to four-component instructional design*. Routledge.

Comprehension strategies are explicit and implicit methods that support active reading, writing, and *discussion* to determine a text's meaning. Through *think alouds,* teachers mirror these cognitive processes, giving students a means for increasing their reading *comprehension* and creating awareness of reading as a learned skill. Applying comprehension strategies helps students become effective problem solvers by giving them the means to dig deeper into challenging texts (Gallagher, 2004; Duke & Pearson, 2009; Schoenbach et al., 2012).

Since productive readers often use comprehension strategies both knowingly and unknowingly (Duke & Pearson, 2009), the development of students' *metacognitive awareness* of their strategic thinking is necessary in order to improve students' **understanding** of when, where, and why they deliberately apply a strategy, or several strategies, in the comprehension of textual meaning (Schoenbach et al., 2012; Pressley & Allington, 2015). To support reading comprehension, teachers must assess students' **background knowledge** in order to decide which comprehension strategies meet the students' academic and cultural *literacy* needs.

Visualizing, *summarizing*, making predictions and inferences, and questioning texts (Duke & Pearson, 2009) are all learned strategies that can increase a readers' comprehension. Teachers should first *explicitly model* comprehension strategies during **guided reading,** whole group instruction, or *collaborative* reading and writing and then *gradually release responsibility* (Pearson & Gallagher, 1983; Duke & Pearson, 2009) of applying strategies to students.

Pressley and Allington (2015, p. 318) found that comprehension strategies become less explicitly taught in upper-level elementary. Having teachers plan intentionally to develop students' metacognition of reading could prompt more **direct instruction** of comprehension strategies. [Contributed by Holly Sheppard Riesco]

Duke, N. K., & Pearson, P. D. (2009). Effective practices for developing reading comprehension. *The Journal of Education, 189*(1/2), 107–122.

Gallagher, K. (2004). *Deeper reading: Comprehending challenging texts, 4–12.* Stenhouse Publishers.

Pearson, P. D., & Gallagher, M. C. (1983). The instruction of reading comprehension. *Contemporary Educational Psychology, 8*(3), 317–344.

Pressley, M., & Allington, R. L. (2015). *Reading instruction that works: The case for balanced teaching* (4th ed.). The Guilford Press.

Schoenbach, R., Greenleaf, C., & Murphy, L. (2012). *Reading for understanding: How reading apprenticeship improves disciplinary learning in secondary and college classrooms* (2nd ed.). Jossey-Bass.

Comprehensive literacy instruction is an approach that includes skill instruction and emphasis on meaning-making through reading/writing, speaking/listening, and viewing/representing (Malloy et al., 2019). Evidence-based best practices suited to students' needs are incorporated through whole-group, *small-group*, and *individualized instruction*. Practices such as *phonics* and word study, *read alouds, modeled and shared reading and writing, guided reading and writing, conferring*, and accountable talk are appropriately proportioned based on developmental needs (Frey et al., 2005).

In comprehensive *literacy* instruction, students are reading to learn as they learn to read. Teachers include a wide variety of increasingly-complex texts to promote *close reading* and *critical thinking* by engaging students in active learning including *annotation, discussion*, and writing with *evidence*. Because of the complexity of reading and the differences among learners and contexts, no single instructional approach has been found to be effective in teaching all students to read (Compton-Lily et al., 2020; Malloy et al., 2019); thus, in comprehensive literacy instruction, teachers monitor and adjust instruction based on formative *assessment.*

The term *balanced literacy,* implying a balance between phonics and meaning, is in widespread use but has been criticized as a synonym for *whole language* or a descriptor of a haphazard approach to literacy instruction (Castles et al., 2018; Snow, 2017). Because many different factors come together in the complex processes of literacy, the term *comprehensive literacy instruction* is more appropriate (Raskinski & Padak, 2004). The guiding principle, according to Castles and colleagues (2018), is that "instructional regimens to support these various abilities are likely to be most effective at particular points in development" (p. 39); however, ongoing attention to literacy's functions and purposes should be maintained. [Contributed by Vicki Stewart Collet]

Castles, A., Rastle, K., & Nation, K. (2018). Ending the reading wars: Reading acquisition from novice to expert. *Psychological Science in the Public Interest, 19*(1), 5–51.

Compton-Lilly, C. F., Mitra, A., Guay, M., & Spence, L. K. (2020). A confluence of complexity: Intersections among reading theory, neuroscience, and observations of young readers. *Reading Research Quarterly, 55,* S185–S195.

Frey, B. B., Lee, S. W., Tollefson, N., Pass, L., & Massengill, D. (2005). Balanced literacy in an urban school district. *Journal of Educational Research, 98*(5), 272–280.

Malloy, J. A., Marinak, B. A., & Gambrell, L. B. (2019). *Best practices in literacy instruction.* Guilford Press.

Rasinski, T., & Padak, N. (2004). Beyond consensus—beyond balance: Toward a comprehensive literacy curriculum. *Reading & Writing Quarterly, 20*(1), 91–102.

Snow, C. E. (2017). The role of vocabulary versus knowledge on children's language learning: A fifty-year perspective. *Journal for the Study of Education and Development, 40,* 1–18.

Construction-Integration (CI) Model is a *discourse-processing* model of reading developed by Kintsch and van Dijk (1978) that views readers as active constructors of meaning and describes different levels of text representation: the *surface level* (letters and words), the *propositional level* (making meaning from words), and the situational level (connecting with *prior experience* and making predictions).

The model theorizes that **comprehension** occurs across two iterative processing stages. During the construction phase, **semantic** *and syntactic information* is used to generate a *literal* interpretation of the text, drawing on related *schemata* in long-term memory. This phase occurs one phrase or sentence at a time, as propositions (small units of meaning) are formed. This phase is typically considered to be a passive one, with more active construction occurring if coherence breaks down (O'Brien & Cook, 2016; Perfetti & Stafura, 2014). During the subsequent integration phase, associations among propositions that are important to the central meaning of the text are strengthened, while associations among less important propositions are minimized or eliminated from the constructed meaning. Propositions must be both relevant and related to survive the integration process (O'Brien & Cook, 2016). *Automatic processes* in the construction phase may provide a head start on comprehension (Perfetti & Stafura, 2014). As reading continues, new information initiates new construction and integration cycles.

The Construction-Integration model predicts what readers will recall after reading a passage and the types of *inferences* that may be made during reading. The CI model is built on the assumption that readers link incoming content with information from previously-read texts and general world knowledge. It explains the interactive combination of top down (knowledge-driven) and bottom up (word-driven) processes (Perfetti & Stafura, 2014). [Contributed by Vicki Stewart Collet]

Kintsch, W., & van Dijk, T. A. (1978). Toward a model of text comprehension and production. *Psychological Review, 85,* 363–394.

O'Brien, E. J., & Cook, A. E. (2016). Separating the activation, integration, and validation components of reading. In B. H. Ross (Ed.), *Psychology of learning and motivation* (pp. 249–276).

Perfetti, C., & Stafura, J. (2014). Word knowledge in a theory of reading comprehension. *Scientific Studies of Reading, 18*(1), 22–37.

Context (after the Latin *contextus* and *contexere,* to join together or interweave) has been described as the language that surrounds a word, idea, or concept. It can also describe the situation of a place or event. More implicitly, it is details of who, what, where, and why that help an individual understand the meaning and relevancy of the whole (Bloome, 1985).

Context involves knowing how language is used and how to use language. It is not only about which words are chosen, either in written or oral form, but how they are arranged. The meaning of a word can also change depending on what others surround it. Together these elements create an integrated framework to convey and understand the objective and purpose of a message (Goodman & Goodman, 2019). In teaching, context connects instructional practices to students' prior knowledge and lived experiences,

Social context, in particular, refers to a specific *setting* or set of circumstances in which individuals interact. For example, in the case of a reading group, it would be the where, when, and what is being read (Bloome, 1985). In relation to a professional or academic setting or an informal gathering with friends and family, context would affect word choice, inflection, dialect, and accent as well as mode of delivery and perception.

Students and teachers, on the playground, in the classroom, or at home, will also change their *register* depending on the context (Joos, 1967). In this sense, the context for writing a reflection journal after a coaching session will be distinct from that of a parent-teacher conference. While both are reflective, one describes personal feelings using *symbols* and the other adopts a formal register to discuss a student's academic progress and behavior.

A student, on the other hand, may use *context clues* (e.g., information available) to try to find **understanding** and confirm meaning in a text or conversation. While using hints, strategies, or features (e.g., *inferences*, definitions, examples, graphics, images, illustrations, etc.) is helpful in determining meaning, this is usually not enough (Stahl & Nagy, 2007). Students also need to use **semantics** and **background knowledge** to create meaning if they are going to be able to keep the **discussion** going or continue reading (Stahl & Nagy, 2007). [Contributed by Rebecca Carpenter de Cortina] [See also Sociocultural Perspective, Culturally Responsive Instruction]

Bloome, D. (1985). Reading as a social process. *Language Arts, 62*(2), 134–142.

Goodman, Y. M., & Goodman, K. S. (2019). To ERR is human: Learning about language processes by analyzing miscues. In D. E. Alvermann, N. J. Unrau, M. Sailors, & R. B. Ruddell (Eds.), *Theoretical models and processes of literacy* (7th ed., pp. 146–160). Routledge.

Joos, M. (1967). *The five clocks.* Harcourt, Brace, & World.

Stahl, S. A., & Nagy, W. E. (2007). *Teaching word meanings.* Taylor & Francis Group.

Contextual reading models situate reading as an activity influenced by interactions within a *sociocultural* context. *Context,* in this view, is a broad term that includes not only the words and ideas that surround a word or phrase, but also the *purpose* for reading and the setting where reading occurs. Even more broadly, the social, cultural, and historical settings or situations influence the way readers make meaning of a text. Those with a contextual view of reading consider *literacy* to be a cultural activity because it is acquired through social interaction and is an indication of how a group interprets the world and shares information. Using this lens, the RAND Reading Study Group (Kirby, 2003) defines reading *comprehension* as "the process of simultaneously extracting and constructing meaning through interaction and involvement with written language" (p. 1). In their view, comprehension consists of three elements: the reader, the text, and the activity of reading, all occurring within a larger sociocultural context. They developed a heuristic to show how these elements relate: a circle with these three elements in the center surrounded by a ring of sociocultural context.

The RAND (Kirby, 2003) description of a contextual model for reading considers the cognitive abilities, *motivation,* and knowledge that the reader brings to the text, which vary significantly among readers. Similarly, *textual features* vary widely across *genres* and *modes*. Reading activities include purposes for reading, processes undertaken by the reader, and outcomes of the activity. Outcomes may include increases in knowledge, solutions to problems, and *engagement*. These processes and outcomes are dependent on reader attributes and features of the text. The reader, text, and activity are all influenced by social, cultural, and historical factors. [Contributed by Vicki Stewart Collet] [See also Transactional Theory, Sociocultural Perspective]

Kirby, S. N. (2003). *Developing an R&D program to improve reading comprehension.* RAND Corporation.

Critical literacy is the ability to actively read and produce texts in ways that develop one's ***understanding*** of how power structures can perpetuate issues of inequality and injustice in society. Its "critical" nature is tied to the work of critical theorists, educators, and organizations such as the Frankfurt School of the 1930s, the Birmingham Centre for Contemporary Cultural Studies of the 1960s, Paulo Freire, and Henry Giroux, among others. Critical theory's ultimate aim is "to liberate human beings from the circumstances that enslave them" (Horkheimer, 1982, p. 244).

Similarly, **critical media literacy** is an expanded conception of *literacy* whose aim is to critically analyze relationships between media and audiences, information, and power through exploring various forms of mass communication, popular culture, and new technologies (Kellner & Share, 2007). It is the critical counterpart of *media literacy*, defined as "the ability to access, analyze, evaluate, create, and act using all forms of communication" (NAMLE, n.d.). Media literacy has become increasingly focused on issues of social and environmental justice, to the point where distinctions between "media literacy" and "critical media literacy" have blurred. Yet, a person may demonstrate excellent media literacy skills while lacking awareness of injustices in society perpetuated by power structures, suggesting that distinguishing between the two may still be necessary.

In practice, developing critical (media) literacy can take various forms, such as engaging in "critical conversations" (Shieble et al., 2020), analyzing who is dis/advantaged by the distribution of a particular photograph, news story, or advertisement; listening to and amplifying the voices of those who have been disadvantaged, oppressed, and/or marginalized; and creating counter-narratives that speak back to larger status quo *discourses* through *digital composition*. Critical (media) literacy will remain essential in education as long as it remains essential for all of us to engage "with the ways in which we produce and consume meaning, whose meanings count and whose are dismissed, who speaks and who is silenced, [and] who benefits and who is disadvantaged" (Janks, 2012, p. 159). [Contributed by Seth D. French]

Horkheimer, M. (1982). *Critical theory*. Seabury Press.

Janks, H. (2012). The importance of critical literacy. *English Teaching: Practice and Critique, 11*(1), 150–163.

Kellner, D., & Share, J. (2007). Critical media literacy is not an option. *Learning Inquiry, 1*(1), 59–69.

National Association for Media Literacy Education (NAMLE). (n.d.). *Media literacy defined.* https://namle.net/resources/media-literacy-defined/

Schieble, M., Vetter, A., & Martin, K. M. (2020). *Classroom talk for social change: Critical conversation in English language arts.* Teachers College Press.

Cueing systems are sources of information that may aid in *word identification* and meaning, including **phonics; *morphemic analysis***; and visual, *syntactic*, and **semantic** information.

The cueing systems are linked to Kenneth Goodman's (1967) influential but unfortunately-titled paper, "Reading: A Psychological Guessing Game." More appropriately, reading is viewed as a problem-solving activity, with cueing systems central to that process. *Graphophonic* knowledge works in concert with structure and syntax during **decoding** in both skilled and unskilled readers; moreover, illustrations and other graphic resources are tools for accessing meaning and monitoring meaning construction (Compton-Lily et al., 2020). The three cueing system model (Clay, 2005) includes meaning, structure, and visual (graphophonic) information (MSV) and strongly resembles the ***four-part mental processor*** model (Seidenberg & McClelland, 1989), which suggests that recognizing words requires processing of ***phonological*** and *orthographic information*, context, and meaning. Evidence supports encouraging readers to use everything they know when reading, including when they are decoding unknown words (Duke, 2020; Scanlon & Anderson, 2020).

Some reports have erroneously stated there is not research to support instruction utilizing cueing systems (Hanford, 2019; Petcher et al., 2020; Seidenberg, 2017). However, studies suggest benefits of instructional approaches that encourage interactive and confirmatory use of graphophonic and meaning-based strategies (Scanlon & Anderson, 2020; Wang et al., 2011; Wright & Cervetti, 2017). Additionally, **miscue analysis** (analyzing readers' insertions, omissions, repetitions, reversals, and substitutions based on the cueing systems) gives insight into reading processes that can guide instructional decisions (Clay, 2005). Analysis of cueing systems provides insight on *emerging bilinguals'* use of multiple language and **literacy** resources (Goodman et al., 2005; Noguerón-Liu, 2020), and drawing attention to cues may extend emerging bilinguals' language knowledge and reading skill (Croce, 2015).

Thoroughly attending to the alphabet information in a word is critical for reading but does not preclude the use of other sources of information. Because English orthography is not entirely reliable and some *spelling patterns* have multiple pronunciations and meanings, phonics knowledge alone is insufficient; readers use additional cues to direct and check their word-solving, for both analysis and confirmation (Ehri, 2014; Share 1995; Scanlon & Anderson, 2020). Additionally, including meaning-based decoding strategies encourages learners to understand that the purpose of reading is to construct meaning. Such approaches also allow developing readers to engage in ***independent reading*** sooner by assisting in solving words that include phonics elements they have not yet learned, thus expanding exposure and building word-reading *fluency* (Scanlon & Anderson, 2020). Using phonics and contextual information interactively facilitates the ability to build *sight vocabulary* and construct meaning. [Contributed by Vicki Stewart Collet] [See also Four-Part Mental Processor]

Clay, M. M. (2005). *An observation survey of early literacy achievement* (2nd ed.). Heinemann.

Compton-Lilly, C. F., Mitra, A., Guay, M., & Spence, L. K. (2020). A confluence of complexity: Intersections among reading theory, neuroscience, and observations of young readers. *Reading Research Quarterly, 55*, S185–S195.

Croce, K.-A. (2015). Latino(a) and Burmese elementary school students reading scientific informational texts: The interrelationship of the language of the texts, students' talk, and conceptual change theory. *Linguistics and Education, 29*, 94–106.

Duke, N. (2020). When young readers get stuck. *Educational Leadership, 78*(3), 26–33.

Ehri, L. C. (2014). Orthographic mapping in the acquisition of sight word reading, spelling memory, and vocabulary learning. *Scientific Studies of Reading, 18*(1), 5–21.

Goodman, K. S. (1967). Reading: A psycholinguistic guessing game. *Literacy Research and Instruction, 6*(4), 126–135.

Goodman, Y. M., Watson, D. J., & Burke, C. L. (2005). *Reading miscue inventory: From evaluation to instruction* (2nd ed.). Richard C. Owen.

Hanford, E. (2019, August 22). *At a loss for words: How a flawed idea is teaching millions of kids to be poor readers.* APM Reports.

Noguerón-Liu, S. (2020). Expanding the knowledge base in literacy instruction and assessment: Biliteracy and translanguaging perspectives from families, communities, and classrooms. *Reading Research Quarterly, 55*, S307–S318.

Petscher, Y., Cabell, S. Q., Catts, H. W., Compton, D. L., Foorman, B. R., Hart, S. A., … Wagner, R. K. (2020). How the science of reading informs 21st-century education. *Reading Research Quarterly, 55*, S267–S282.

Scanlon, D. M., & Anderson, K. L. (2020). Using context as an assist in word solving: The contributions of 25 years of research on the interactive strategies approach. *Reading Research Quarterly, 55*, S19–S34.

Seidenberg, M. (2017). *Language at the speed of sight: How we read, why so many can't, and what can be done about it.* Basic.

Seidenberg, M. S., & McClelland, J. L. (1989). A distributed, developmental model of word recognition and naming. *Psychological Review, 96*(4), 523.

Share, D. L. (1995). Phonological recoding and self-teaching: *Sine qua non* of reading acquisition. *Cognition, 55*(2), 151–218.

Wang, H.-C., Castles, A., Nickels, L., & Nation, K. (2011). Context effects on orthographic learning of regular and irregular words. *Journal of Experimental Child Psychology, 109*(1), 39–57.

Wright, T. S., & Cervetti, G. N. (2017). A systematic review of the research on vocabulary instruction that impacts text comprehension. *Reading Research Quarterly, 52*(2), 203–226.

Culturally responsive instruction is defined as "using the cultural characteristics, experiences, and *perspectives* of ethnically *diverse* students as conduits for teaching them more effectively" (Gay, 2002, p. 106). Culturally responsive instruction is often used synonymously with culturally relevant pedagogy, a term first coined by Gloria Ladson-Billings in 1995. Within the overall framework of culturally responsive teaching that seeks to build bridges between the students' home culture and that of the school, students need to experience academic success, develop and maintain cultural competence, and develop critical consciousness through which they actively challenge the status quo (Ladson-Billings, 1995). It is a pedagogy that supports teaching to and through each student's unique *funds of knowledge* (Moll et al., 1992). By connecting home and school communities, students' unique cultures and social capital are acknowledged and valued (Brown-Jeffy & Cooper, 2011). An expansion of *equity* and access of students and communities of color can lead to a reimagining of schools where "diverse, heterogeneous practices are not only valued but *sustained*" (Paris & Alim 2017, p. 3).

The implementation of culturally responsive instruction includes the use of *multicultural texts* to provide differing perspectives, the addition of *multiliteracies* in acquiring new information, creating curriculum that builds on the unique strengths of each student and, most importantly, cultivating an environment of belonging through positive relationships. Being culturally responsive also acknowledges that students may learn and demonstrate their learning in *multimodal* ways (Greiner, 2020). Culturally responsive literacy instruction should serve to validate students' *identities* and ways of knowing, engage students through relevancy and purpose, and empower students as readers and writers (Ruday, 2019). [Contributed by Angelia C. Greiner]

Brown-Jeffy, S., & Cooper, J. E. (2011). Toward a conceptual framework of culturally relevant pedagogy: An overview of the conceptual and theoretical literature. *Teacher Education Quarterly*, 65–84.

Gay, G. (2002). Preparing for culturally responsive teaching. *Journal of Teacher Education, 53*(2), 106–116.

Greiner, A. C. (2020). *Culturally responsive pedagogy and writing achievement for native high school students* [Unpublished doctoral dissertation]. University of Arkansas.

Ladson-Billing, G. (1995). Toward a theory of culturally relevant pedagogy. *American Educational Research Journal, 32*(3), 465–491.

Moll, L. C., Amanti, C., Neff, D., & Gonzalez, N. (1992). Funds of knowledge for teaching: Using a qualitative approach to connect homes and classrooms. *Theory into Practice, 31*(2), 132–141.

Paris, D., & Alim, H. S. (Eds.). (2017). *Culturally sustaining pedagogies: Teaching and learning for justice in a changing world.* Teachers College Press.

Ruday, S. (2019). *Culturally relevant teaching in the English language arts classroom.* Routledge.

Decoding is the process of translating the visual *symbols* of a writing system that represent the spoken language within a reader's culture (Ziegler & Goswami, 2005).

In alphabetic *orthographies*, such as English, decoding connects letters (*graphemes*) to sounds (*phonemes*) in written words using pronunciations to get words into a reader's memory to be read later automatically by sight. The acquisition of this alphabetic knowledge of connecting graphemes to phonemes transports a reader through four alphabetic phases (Ehri, 2020). A reader in the pre-alphabetic phase does not use decoding, but instead uses visual and contextual knowledge of words. A reader has moved into the partial alphabetic phase when able to use some decoding, such as letter names and/or sounds. Once a reader is able to decode, by analyzing and connecting graphemes and phonemes within unknown words, the reader has moved into the full alphabetic phase. Finally, when a reader has knowledge of larger consolidated *spelling patterns* representing spoken *syllables* and *morphemes* and can use these larger units to decode unknown multi-syllabic words, the reader has moved into the consolidated alphabetic phase.

Decoding is necessary but not sufficient for reading; decoding and ***comprehension*** are both crucial (Gough & Tunmer, 1986). For true reading to occur, words that are decoded must also be understood by the reader.

Decodable text is instructional text that purposefully contains an abundance of phonetically regular words with a grapheme-phoneme combination that has been previously taught to the reader. There is not an agreed upon number nor percentage of decodable words that qualifies a text as decodable (Cheatham & Allor, 2012).

Encoding, or *spelling*, is the opposite process from decoding and uses grapheme-phoneme connections to transform spoken language into visual symbols. [Contributed by Wyann Stanton] [See also Dyslexia; Sight Words]

Ehri, L. C. (2020). The science of learning to read words: A case for systematic phonics instruction. *Reading Research Quarterly, 55*(S1), S45–S60.

Cheatham, J. P., & Allor, J. H. (2012). The influence of decodability in early reading text on reading achievement: A review of the evidence. *Reading and Writing,* 25(9), 2223–2246.

Gough, P. B., & Tunmer, W. E. (1986). Decoding, reading, and reading disability. *Remedial and Special Education,* 7(1), 6–10.

Ziegler, J. C., & Goswami, U. (2005). Reading acquisition, developmental dyslexia, and skilled reading across languages: A psycholinguistic grain size theory. *Psychological Bulletin, 131*(1), 3.

Differentiation is a way of thinking about teaching and learning that responds to students' individual differences by refining the curriculum to best suit each student's unique learning needs (Tomlinson, 2000). When instruction is differentiated it is uniquely designed for a specific learner or group of learners to enhance their acquisition of skills, concepts, and strategies.

World-renowned expert on differentiation, Carol Ann Tomlinson (2000), outlines the following seven beliefs on which differentiation operates:

– Students who are the same age differ in their readiness to learn, their interests, their styles of learning, their experiences, and their life circumstances.
– The differences in students are significant enough to make a major impact on what students need to learn, the pace at which they need to learn it, and the support they need from teachers and others to learn it well.
– Students will learn best when supportive adults push them slightly beyond where they can work without assistance.
– Students will learn best when they can make a connection between the curriculum and their interests and life experiences.
– Students will learn best when learning opportunities are natural.
– Students are more effective learners when classrooms and schools create a sense of community in which students feel significant and respected.
– The central job of schools is to maximize the capacity of each student (pp. 6–7).

Differentiation is inherently resistant to the *standardization of curriculum* and instruction because attempts to standardize often ignore the *diversity* of learners present; for example, teachers may be required to focus on short texts vs. longer texts or novels (Shelton & Brooks, 2019). In contrast, educators employing differentiation in their classrooms personalize their curriculum and instruction through *small-group learning experiences*, paired reading opportunities, assignments with various difficulty levels, student choice in the process and product of assignments, opportunities for independent research suited to students' varied interests, and other *student-centered* strategies whose goal is to uniquely engage each student as they build mastery over the content (Tomlinson, 2008). [Contributed by Seth D. French] [see also Guided Reading; Intervention]

Shelton, S. A., & Brooks, T. (2019). "We need to get these scores up": A narrative examination of the challenges of teaching literature in the age of standardized testing. *Journal of Language and Literacy Education, 15*(2), 1–17.
Tomlinson, C. A. (2000). Reconcilable differences: Standards-based teaching and differentiation. *Educational Leadership, 58*(1), 6–13.
Tomlinson, C. A. (2008). The goals of differentiation. *Educational Leadership, 66*(3), 26–30.

Digital literacies refer to the plural *literacies* needed to manage information and communication in the ever-evolving and increasingly digital world of the 21st century. Notice the plural "literacies" in keeping with the *sociocultural perspective* on *literacy* as practice, which holds that literacies should be conceptualized as plural rather than singular (Lankshear & Knobel, 2008).

Creating a definition for digital literacies that is both concise and all-encompassing is challenging—if not altogether impossible—due to their complex and multifaceted nature. Lankshear and Knobel (2008) have noted this, pointing to examples such as ICT/computer literacy, information literacy, technological literacy, *media literacy*, communication literacy, e-literacy, digital competence, and others to illustrate the need for specificity when discussing digital literacies.

What it means to be "digitally literate" is also complex. To some, the digitally literate person is adept in navigating multiple media, tailoring their message and analyses to suit the medium being used. To others, the digitally literate person possesses the ability to perform certain tasks and skills deemed "standard" to navigate and utilize the digital technologies available to them (Lankshear & Knobel, 2008). Because digital technologies are rapidly evolving, even the most digitally literate among us could be considered virtually inept within a few years if they did not take the time to familiarize themselves with current digital technologies and nurture their abilities to successfully navigate them. It's important to note that the use of certain digital tools and apps serves to mediate literacy learning in ways that are different from print literacies, particularly in terms of processes for reading digital texts (Coiro, 2021).

Finally, digital literacies must consider the importance of *criticality, understanding* how the texts we consume and produce in digital spaces favor some *perspectives* while marginalizing or excluding others (Gillen, 2014). The New London Group's (1996) emphasis on critical framing and transformed practice within "*multiliteracies*" is instructive as we consider how digital literacies enable us to critically analyze the social contexts in which we live and become designers of social futures ourselves. [Contributed by Seth D. French] [see also Multimodality; New Literacies]

Coiro, J. (2021). Toward a multifaceted heuristic of digital reading to inform assessment, research, practice, and policy. *Reading Research Quarterly, 56*(1), 9–31.

Gillen, J. (2014). *Digital literacies*. Routledge.

Lankshear, C., & Knobel, M. (Eds.). (2008). *Digital literacies: Concepts, policies, and practices*. Peter Lang.

New London Group. (1996). A pedagogy of multiliteracies: Designing social futures. *Harvard Educational Review, 66*, 60–92.

Direct instruction, or *explicit instruction*, "...is an instructional model that focuses on the interaction between teachers and students" (Magliaro, Lockhee, & Burton, 2005, p. 41). The goal of direct instruction is to achieve basic skill mastery through **modeling**, corrective *feedback*, reinforcement, and practice (Engleman et al., 1988). Underlying assumptions are that with the instructor as the director of all activities, students will learn more in less time while addressing a variety of achievement levels (Engleman et al., 1988). Typically associated with *scripted curriculum* design, over the last thirty-plus years, some direct instruction models have been designed to include strategy instruction in addition to skill mastery (Magliaro et al., 2005; Rupley, Blair, & Nichols, 2009). Later models incorporate *"think-alouds"* as a key component of strategy acquisition and are less rigid in instructional *design* (Magliaro et al., 2005; Rupley et al., 2009).

Originally based on the tenets of behaviorism (Engleman et al., 1988), later models incorporate *schema theory* (Rupley et al., 2009), automatic information processing theory (LaBerge & Samuels, 1974; Rupley et al., 2009), and the **Gradual Release of Responsibility** model (Pearson & Gallagher, 1983; Rupley et al., 2009). The incorporation of such theories promote flexibility in direct instructional design as suggested by Rupley, Blair, and Nichols (2009), "Skill learning requires more control and direction by the teacher than does strategy learning, which requires less teacher directness and is more under the control of students" (p. 127). Although the direct instruction model has undergone several modifications, it still "...maintains the central purpose of promoting student on-task behavior through explicit instruction, ongoing support, and student engagement in successful practice" (Magliaro et al., 2005, p. 51). [Contributed by Judy L. Fields]

Engelmann, S., Becker, W. C., Carnine, D., & Gersten, R. (1988). The direct instruction follow through model: Design and outcomes. *Education and Treatment of Children, 303–317.*

LaBerge, D., & Samuels, S. J. (1974). Toward a theory of automatic information processing in reading. *Cognitive Psychology, 6*(2), 293–323.

Magliaro, S. G., Lockee, B. B., & Burton, J. K. (2005). Direct instruction revisited: A key model for instructional technology. *Educational Technology Research and Development, 53*(4), 41–55.

Pearson, P. D., & Gallagher, M. C. (1983). The instruction of reading comprehension. *Contemporary Educational Psychology, 8*(3), 317–344.

Rupley, W. H., Blair, T. R., & Nichols, W. D. (2009). Effective reading instruction for struggling readers: The role of direct/explicit teaching. *Reading & Writing Quarterly, 25*(2–3), 125–138.

Disciplinary literacy, often mistaken for *content knowledge*, engages students in the *literacy* norms, values, and strategies within a particular discipline. Research suggests that disciplines have unique ways of thinking about problems that impact the literacy practices within that specific field (Shanahan & Shanahan, 2008); therefore, students need to develop an awareness of the literacy practices within a discipline (Wolsey & Lapp, 2017).

Instruction in disciplinary literacy introduces students to the reading, writing, and communicative styles that the discipline favors. Disciplinary literacy instruction centers students in a social, *collaborative* literacy (Moje, 2015) that moves them from spectators of content to active participants in meaning-making through literacy practices. Rather than compliantly learning the subject's content, students enact their curiosity to construct knowledge by mirroring the analytical, interpretive, or creative practices of experts within the field (Shanahan & Shanahan, 2008). Students develop an awareness of disciplinary culture and *discourse* (Moje, 2015) and engage in the field's organizational language and literacy structures (Wolsey & Lapp, 2017).

In an approach to effective disciplinary literacy instruction, students may consider inquiry-based problems within the discipline and learn to collect data through *content-area reading and writing* practices to solve problems. Further, the data collection's *purpose* and *audience* are inextricably linked to students' development of disciplinary literacy **understandings** (Moje, 2015). By asking students to consider various purposes and audiences, instructors welcome students' involvement in disciplinary issues through an insider **perspective.** Moreover, in determining how to create solutions for a particular audience and purpose, students interpret the content through reasoning and synthesis of sources to construct meaning, rather than accepting meaning passively.

For example, disciplinary literacy in English language arts (ELA) encourages students' curiosity, inquiry, and solution-oriented skills by tackling social justice topics, such as systemic racism and climate change, through interdisciplinary **discussion,** reading, and writing. Disciplinary literacy in ELA enables students' critical consciousness (Freire, 1970) and supports students' transformative acts within and beyond communities of discourse. [Contributed by Holly Sheppard Riesco]

Freire, P. (1970). *Pedagogy of the oppressed*. Bloomsbury Academic.

Moje, E. B. (2015). Doing and teaching disciplinary literacy with adolescent learners: A social and cultural enterprise. *Harvard Educational Review, 85*(2), 254–278.

Shanahan, T., & Shanahan, C. (2008). Teaching disciplinary literacy to adolescents: Rethinking content-area literacy. *Harvard Educational Review, 78*(1), 40–59.

Wolsey, T. D., & Lapp, D. (2017). *Literacy in the disciplines: A teacher's guide*. The Guilford Press.

Discourse analysis considers language use as social practice and the ways in which language reflects and constructs the social world. Although the meaning of *discourse* may seem apparent—talk, speech, language—discourse means much more than words, whether written or spoken. Through *internally persuasive discourse* (Bakhtin, 1981), worldviews are constructed. Discourse plays an essential role in education: Unlike other institutions, which may serve their clients in nonlinguistic ways, schools function largely through communication. Classroom discourse is a tool for sharing ideas, maintaining social relationships, and expressing *identities* (Cazden, 2001).

Discourse analysis draws from many fields, including anthropology, linguistics, and psychology. Some discourse analysts focus on discourse as the spoken work transcribed carefully to hear minute differences. Others focus on spoken interaction among individuals and groups, looking closely at turns and topic construction. Still others focus on discourse more broadly, considering norms of speech, thought, and action in various domains, and yet others focus on analysis of the written word and digital domains, including *multimodal* composition. As a tool for educational research, discourse analysis has been used to examine the way people make meaning in educational contexts.

Critical discourse analysis (CDA) is "an attempt to bring social theory and discourse analysis together to describe, interpret, and explain the ways in which discourse constructs, becomes constructed by, represents, and becomes represented by the social world" (Rogers et al., 2005, p. 366). CDA seeks to explain why and how language does the work that it does. For education researchers in the United States, Gee's (1999) theory of discourse has been influential and reflects a critical stance, claiming that all discourses are ideological and that some are valued more than others, representing power relations. His theory distinguishes between "little d" and "Big D" discourses, with the former referring to linguistic elements and the latter referring to both language bits and the cultural models associated with them. Analysis of classroom discourse opens possibilities for **understanding** how social relations may be resisted and transformed. [Contributed by Vicki Stewart Collet] [See also Critical Literacy]

Bakhtin, M. (1981). *The dialogic imagination: Four essays.* University of Texas Press.

Cazden, C. B. (2001). *Classroom discourse: The language of teaching and learning.* Heinemann.

Gee, J. P. (1999). *An introduction to discourse analysis.* Routledge.

Rogers, R., Malancharuvil-Berkes, E., Mosley, M. Hui, D., & Joseph, G. O. (2005). Critical discourse analysis in education. *Review of Educational Research, 75*(3), 365–416.

Discussion is the verbal exchange of ideas in a learning environment. Also referred to in educational settings as *classroom talk*, it involves the exploration of ideas among students and teachers in conversation with each other. Relative to *literacy* instruction, it often centers on the texts students have read, as a means for connecting content with students' lived experiences or with other texts. Essentially, discussion seeks to expand learning beyond basic *comprehension* of texts and into higher-level thinking and application.

Discussions in literacy settings exhibit characteristics of that context's *discourse*, described as the customary or accepted manner in which members within a certain group or community should think, feel, or talk (Gee, 2008). In the classroom, these expectations are formed as teachers and students establish the criteria for *productive talk*. Classroom discussions often follow an initiation–response–evaluation pattern (IRE), putting the teacher at the center of the discussion (Cazden, 1988). To shift the discourse and instead make discussions more student-driven and centered on student thinking, literacy educators can consider ways to structure discussions where students are the arbiters of knowledge and are building on their *peers'* ideas. One example of this is the *Socratic seminar*, in which students prepare and ask questions centered on a text and respond critically to each other in an open discussion forum (Tredway, 1995).

Effective student discussions include *dialogue*, or the sharing of ideas that respond to what others have said. Bakhtin (1981) suggests that new ideas and *understandings* are created as a variety of voices are given space to participate in learning dialogues and co-construct knowledge. Dialogic student discussions exhibit exploration of ideas, reasoned explanations, intertextual connections, authentic questioning, and overall uptake of others' ideas (Soter et al., 2008). Discussions like these provide space for students to question, to explore, to present new *perspectives*. [Contributed by Johnny B. Allred]

Bakhtin, M. (1981). *The dialogic imagination: Four essays by M. M. Bakhtin* (C. Emerson & M. Holquist, Trans.). University of Texas Press.

Cazden, C. B. (1988). *Classroom discourse: The language of teaching and learning*. Heinemann.

Gee, J. P. (2008). *Social linguistics and literacies: Ideology in discourses* (3rd ed.). Routledge.

Soter, A. O., Wilkinson, I. A., Murphy, P. K., Rudge, L., Reninger, K., & Edwards, M. (2008). What the discourse tells us: Talk and indicators of high-level comprehension. *International Journal of Educational Research, 47*(6), 372–391.

Treadway, L. (1995). Socratic seminars: Engaging students in intellectual discourse. *Educational Leadership, 53*(1), 26–29.

Dyslexia is a severe difficulty in *decoding* the printed words of a language (Vellutino et al., 2004). Controversy surrounds dyslexia, including the usefulness of the term. Some believe dyslexia to be a distinct disorder (IDA, 2016), while others believe there is no empirical foundation for categorizing one group as different from others with severe reading difficulties (ILA, 2016).

Dyslexia has no universally accepted definition nor consistent guidelines for a definitive diagnosis, yet there are some points of convergence (IDA, 2016; ILA, 2016; Worthy, 2018). There are some students who, regardless of intelligence and creativity, have reading acquisition difficulties which are not due to gender, general learning disabilities, nor extraneous factors such as sensory acuity deficits, socioeconomic disadvantages, or like factors. These difficulties do not result from visual problems producing letter or word reversals. In addition, clumsiness, fine motor problems, attention deficits, creativity, and handedness are not indicators nor predictors of the difficulty. The most commonly accepted distinguishing characteristic of these severe reading difficulties is a core *phonological* processing deficit in analyzing and manipulating sounds in words that manifests with the inability to decode words accurately and *fluently*, which can lead to secondary characteristics of problems with *spelling* of words, word recall, *vocabulary*, reading *comprehension, background knowledge, written expression* and/or *motivation* (IDA, 2016; ILA, 2016; Lyon, 2003; Worthy, 2018).

Some of the many points of debate include: the best instructional method, the role of *phonics,* the role of *scripted programs,* the neurobiological and heritability origins of dyslexia, and the term itself (IDA, 2016; ILA, 2016).

The use of early *intervention* that is responsive to the instructional needs of these students is key to changing their trajectory with reading difficulty. [Contributed by Wyann Stanton] [See also Decoding; Intervention]

International Dyslexia Association. (2016). *IDA urges ILA to review and clarify key points in dyslexia research advisory.* https://dyslexiaida.org/ida-urges-ila-to-review-and-clarify-key-points-in-dyslexia-research-advisory/

International Literacy Association. (2016). *Research advisory addendum: Dyslexia: Response to the International Dyslexia Association.* https://literacyworldwide.org/docs/default-source/where-we-stand/ila-dyslexia-research-advisory-addendum.pdf

Lyon, G. R., Shaywitz, S. E., & Shaywitz, B. A. (2003). A definition of dyslexia. *Annals of Dyslexia, 53*(1), 1–14.

Vellutino, F. R., Fletcher, J. M., Snowling, M. J., & Scanlon, D. M. (2004). Specific reading disability (dyslexia): What have we learned in the past four decades? *Journal of Child Psychology and Psychiatry, 45*(1), 2–40.

Worthy, J., Salmerón, C., Long, S. L., Lammert, C., & Godfrey, V. (2018). "Wrestling with the politics and ideology": Teacher educators' responses to dyslexia discourse and legislation. *Literacy Research: Theory, Method, and Practice, 67*(1), 377–393.

Embodied literacies are the construction of textual meaning through bodily activity. In an embodied literacies *perspective, literacy* experiences are seen as physicalized rather than being associated with the mind alone (Lindgren & Johnson-Glenberg, 2013). This post-humanist perspective on literacy practices acknowledges the increasingly multimodal nature of literacies that makes the embodied nature of learning difficult to ignore (Gee, 2004). The concept of embodied literacies moves beyond parsing modes into sensory categories, instead considering an integrated corporal experience and how moving, feeling bodies influence meaning-making.

Words, phrases, and *symbols* "become meaningful through how we perceive and interact with the objects and situations those symbols denote" (Glenberg, 2010, p. 587). Authentic literacy experiences may include feeling, sensing, and moving (Barsalou, 2008). However, in-school literacy learning sometimes confines participation, asking students to "check their bodies at the schoolroom door" (Gee, 2004, p. 39). Research suggests an embodied approach increases literacy learning. For example, activities that pair *oral* English with movement, gesture, and expression foster *English **language development*** and concept acquisition (Capone & McGregor, 2004; Greenfader et al., 2014). Mages (2006) found that including *drama*, using bodies and voices to express characters' actions, solidifies ***comprehension.***

The concept of embodiment has physiological underpinnings—there are neural cells in tissues throughout our body (Siegel, 2010). Although more attention has turned to embodied literacies in recent decades, the idea of embodiment is not new. William James (1890) wrote that "we sense our bodily selves as the seat of our thinking" (cited in Rosenblatt, 1989, p. 245). [Contributed by Vicki Stewart Collet]

Barsalou, L. W. (2008). Grounded cognition. *Annual Review of Psychology, 59,* 617–645.

Capone, N. C., & McGregor, K. K. (2004). Gesture development: A review for clinical and research practices. *Journal of Speech, Language, and Hearing Research, 47*(1), 173–186.

Gee, J. P. (2004). *Situated language and learning.* Routledge.

Glenberg, A. M. (2010). Embodiment as a unifying perspective for psychology. *Wiley Interdisciplinary Reviews: Cognitive Science, 1*(4), 586–596.

Greenfader, C. M., Brouillette, L., & Farkus, G. (2014). Effect of a performing arts program on the oral language skills of young English Learners. *Reading Research Quarterly, 50*(2), 185–203.

Lindgren, R., & Johnson-Glenberg, M. (2013). Emboldened by embodiment: Six precepts for research on embodied learning and mixed reality. *Educational Researcher, 42*(3), 445–452.

Mages, W. K. (2006). Drama and imagination: A cognitive theory of drama's effect on narrative comprehension. *Research in Drama Education, 11*(3), 329–340.

Rosenblatt, L. M. (1989). Writing and reading transactional theory. In J. Mason (Ed.), *Reading and writing connections* (pp. 153–176). Allyn & Bacon.

Siegel, D. J. (2010). *Mindsight: The new science of personal transformation.* Bantam Books.

Emergent literacy includes children's concepts, dispositions, and behaviors about reading and writing before they develop conventional *literacy* (Teale & Sulzby, 1986.) This end of the literacy development continuum involves three critical skills: *oral language development,* concepts about print, and *phonological awareness* (Whitehurst & Lonigan, 1998). Children's experiences with literacy before formal reading instruction are an important part of their overall literacy development. Pioneers in literacy research and education support the idea that learning to read is a process of socialization (Israel & Monaghan, 2007). This process begins as soon as children interact with others.

Often instruction in emergent literacy involves a play-based approach that allows children to explore *receptive* and *expressive* language, environmental print, and the sound systems of language. Building *vocabulary* through oral language exchanges with more knowledgeable others supports future reading by helping children make sense of texts and make connections between texts and their own experiences (Cazden, 2005). *Concepts about print* refers to everything a child knows about how language is written. Awareness often begins with *environmental print* (print that children encounter in their environment in meaningful ways: the cereal box they see every morning, the business signs they pass on the way to school, etc.) As children become aware that written words are *symbolic* representations, they begin to make meaningful marks and attempt to read (Clay, 1989). Children begin to notice and name the sounds of their language during emergent literacy activities including, songs, poems, fingerplays and games. Children's increased skill in *phonological awareness (awareness of the sound structure of language)* is linked with increased skill in *decoding.* The sound system of a language is key to decoding and *encoding* texts and, unlike oral language, must be taught. [Contributed by Savanna L. Gragg]

Cazden, C. (2005). The value of conversations for language development and reading comprehension. *Literacy Teaching and Learning, 9*(1), 1–6.

Clay, M. (1989). Concepts about print in English and other languages. *The Reading Teacher, 42*(4), 268–276.

Israel, S. E., & Monaghan, E. J. (Eds.). (2007). *Shaping the reading field: The impact of early reading pioneers, scientific research, and progressive ideas.* International Reading Association.

Teale, W. H., & Sulzby, E. (1986). *Emergent literacy: Writing and reading* (Writing research: Multidisciplinary inquiries into the nature of writing series). Ablex Publishing Corporation.

Whitehurst, G. J., & Lonigan, C. J. (1998). Child development and emergent literacy. *Child Development, 69*(3), 848–872.

Fluency is "...the ability of readers to read the words in text effortlessly and efficiently (*automaticity*) with meaningful expression that enhances the meaning of the text (prosody)" (Rasinski, 2010, pp. 31–32). The three key elements of fluency are rate (automaticity), accuracy, and prosody. As the elements of fluency work in tandem, the reader is able to move fluidly through connected text with good ***comprehension*** (Rasinski, 2010; Samuels & Farstrup, 2006). Fluency "...is a factor in both oral and *silent reading* that can limit or support comprehension" (Kuhn et al., 2010, p. 240).

Rate is the total number of words read in an established amount of time and can be measured with an oral or silent reading. Automaticity, how quickly the reader *decodes*, reflects the reader's *word recognition* skill (Rasinski, 2010; Samuels & Farstrup, 2006).

Accuracy is typically calculated after an *oral reading* and reported as words correct per minute (wcpm). The number of words read correctly (accuracy) are divided by the total number of words read (rate) and often expressed as a percentage. Rasinski (2010) offers three categories that provide information about a reader's ability to successfully decode a text as follows: 1) Independent Level—99–100% accuracy; 2) Instructional Level—92–98% accuracy; 3) Frustration Level—below 92% accuracy. These categories may inform appropriate instruction (Rasinski, 2010, p. 182). When word-level reading is both automatic and accurate at an appropriate rate, the reader is able to decode text with little cognitive effort (Samuels & Farstrup, 2006).

"*Prosody* is a linguistic term that describes the rhythmic and tonal aspects of speech: the 'music' of oral language" (Samuels & Farstrup, 2006, p. 134) and is evaluated using a descriptive *rubric* that includes *syntactic* phrasing, rhythm, pauses, intonation, and expression that facilitate the comprehension of text more accurately than being able to quickly decode words on a page (Henry & Jackson, 2017). Good prosodic reading mimics speech and potentially supports comprehension (Henry & Jackson, 2017; Kuhn et al., 2010). Fluency develops through extensive reading, *repeated reading, readers' theater, choral reading,* and ***modeling*** (Rasinski, 2010). [Contributed by Judy L. Fields]

Henry, N., & Jackson, C. (2017). The role of prosody and explicit instruction in processing instruction. *The Modern Language Journal, 101*(2), 294–314.

Kuhn, Melanie R., Schwanenflugel, Paula J., & Meisinger, Elizabeth B. (2010). Aligning theory and assessment of reading fluency: Automaticity, prosody, and definitions of fluency. *Reading Research Quarterly, 45*(2), 230–251.

Rasinski, T. V. (2010). *The fluent reader*. Scholastic.

Samuels, S., & Farstrup, A. E. (2006). *What research has to say about fluency instruction.* International Reading Association.

Four-Part Mental Processor is a theoretical explanation of processes involved in *decoding* unfamiliar words (Seidenberg & McClelland, 1989). The four parts are the *phonological* processor, the *orthographic* processor, the meaning processor, and the *context* processor. The phonological processor detects, recalls, and understands the *phonemes* that make up spoken words. The orthographic processor recognizes, stores, and recalls letters and letter combinations for efficient retrieval when reading and *spelling* words. The meaning processor interprets word meanings, categories, and concepts. The context processor supports meaning by interpreting words based on circumstances and *background knowledge* (Moats & Tolman, 2019).

The Four-Part Mental Processing model describes a sequence where phonological and orthographic processors work together to decode a word, after which *vocabulary* knowledge is accessed through the meaning processor. The context processor then determines the appropriate meaning for the word in the situation at hand. The four-part mental processor model resembles the three *cueing systems* model (Clay, 2005); a primary difference is the specified sequential nature of the Four-Part Mental Processing model. Proponents of the Four-Part Mental Processing model often suggest that instruction should also follow this sequence, with *systematic* **phonics** *instruction* as the primary focus, especially for students who struggle with *word identification* (Moats & Tolman, 2019; OSE; 2010; however, see Ellis & Moss, 2014, and Torgerson et al., 2019, for concerns regarding this recommendation). Such approaches purport that students need *explicit* support to understand *phonology* and orthography before moving on to consider meaning and context (Shaywitz, 2003). Alternative views encourage interactive use of and instruction in multiple *cueing systems*. [Contributed by Vicki Stewart Collet] [See also Cueing Systems]

Clay, M. M. (2005). *An observation survey of early literacy achievement* (2nd ed.). Heinemann.

Ellis, S., & Moss, G. (2014). Ethics, education policy and research: The phonics question reconsidered. *British Educational Research Journal, 40*(2), 241–260.

Moats, L. C., & Tolman, C. A. (2019). The challenge of learning to read. *LETRS,* Vol. 1. Voyager Sopris Learning.

Office for Standards in Education. (2010). *Reading by six: How the best schools do it.* Ofsted.

Seidenberg, M. S., & McClelland, J. L. (1989). A distributed, developmental model of word recognition and naming. *Psychological Review, 96*(4), 523.

Shaywitz, S. (2003). *Overcoming dyslexia: A new and complete science-based program for reading programs at any level.* Vintage Books.

Torgerson, C., Brooks, G., Gascoine, L., & Higgins, S. (2019). Phonics: Reading policy and the evidence of effectiveness from a systematic 'tertiary' review. *Research Papers in Education, 34*(2), 208–238.

Genre has become an increasingly nuanced term used to refer to modes of discourse, including but not limited to the written word. As a system of classification, genre categorizes written, spoken, and visual discourses (Frow, 2015). Familiarization with genres provides access to various discourse communities and a better ***understanding*** of authorial intent and purpose.

Understanding of genre increases awareness of an author's or artist's creative choices and the ability to analyze and interpret those choices, specifically how content is connected and how it is relevant (Gee, 2014). New discourse communities and modes of discourse have created new genres that extend beyond traditional literary and written texts, and it is important to examine visual and oral genres alongside written genres. An expanded definition of genre, which includes online and digital texts such as Tweets, memes, and podcasts, allows teachers and students to recognize that social constructs shape elements of genre (Collin, 2012).

Genre situates a text and/or an author within a specific discourse community and reflects the values, motives, and purpose of the text and its creator. For example, the five-paragraph essay is a common written genre in secondary schools and university composition classrooms that seeks to streamline the process of writing for students. This particular genre does not take into account a student's preferred or familiar discourse community but rather asks the student to adhere to a specific type of academic discourse characterized by specific conventions and constraints. This same concept of adhering to discourse conventions can also be applied to visual and spoken genres (Gee, 2014).

Although genre is a relatively new term within pedagogy and composition research (Tardy, 2020), its application in the classroom may have lasting effects on students. Examining genre increases social and linguistic awareness both inside and outside of the classroom (Tardy, 2020). When students have a working understanding of genre, they are afforded access to a wider range of discourse communities and, by extension, become more aware of social conventions and constructions and how to navigate them. [Contributed by Megan Yates Grizzle]

Collin, R. (2012). Genre in discourse, discourse in genre: A new approach to the study of literate practice. *Journal of Literary Research, 44*(1), 76–96.

Frow, J. (2015). *Genre* (2nd ed.). Routledge.

Gee, J. P. (2014). *An introduction to discourse analysis: Theory and method* (3rd ed.). Routledge.

Tardy, C. M., Sommer-Farias, B., & Gevers, J. (2020). Teaching and researching genre knowledge: Toward an enhanced theoretical framework. *Composition Forum, 37*(3), 287–321.

Gradual Release of Responsibility (GRR) is a model for learning that describes how the responsibility for performing a task gradually shifts over time from teacher to student. By providing maximum support initially, the learner's task is simplified as the learner gains competence. Through a sequence of explanation, guided practice, corrective feedback, and independent practice and application, students become independent with tasks that are within their *zone of proximal development* (Pearson & Gallagher, 1983). This *scaffolding* helps a learner navigate the terrain between performing a strategy with support and utilizing the strategy independently. According to Pearson and Gallagher, any academic task can be conceptualized as requiring differing proportions of teacher and learner responsibility for successful completion.

GRR was first offered as a model to describe instruction in reading *comprehension,* and it is often used for daily lesson design: the day's reading instruction may start with whole group, explicit instruction about a strategy—inferring, for instance. This is often followed by the teacher *modeling* or *thinking aloud* about making inferences with a student text. Next, students are asked to do some guided practice, making inferences in the text selection for the day. Finally, there is the assumption that students will use the strategy (make inferences) while reading independently; often *independent reading time* is offered during the school day for this purpose. The GRR can also be used to guide a long-term model for instruction, were teachers change their support of strategy use not just within particular lessons but also across time. Research by Pearson and others has described the GRR model in this way, as a depiction of change over time, a long-term plan for moving students toward independence (Clark & Graves, 2004; Collet, 2012; Dole, Duffy, Roehler & Pearson, 1991; Frey & Fisher, 2010; Kong & Pearson, 2003). [Contributed by Vicki Stewart Collet] [See also Scaffolding]

Clark, K., & Graves, M. (2004). Scaffolding students' comprehension of text. *The Reading Teacher, 58*(6), 570–580.

Collet, V. S. (2012). The gradual increase of responsibility model: Coaching for teacher change. *Literacy Research and Instruction, 51*(1), 27–47.

Dole, J., Duffy, G., Roehler, L., & Pearson, P. D. (1991). Moving from the old to the new: Research on reading comprehension instruction. *Review of Educational Research, 61*(2), 239–264.

Frey, N., & Fisher, D. (2010). Identifying instructional moves during guided learning. *The Reading Teacher, 64*(2), 84–95.

Kong, A., & Pearson, P. D. (2003). The road to participation: The construction of a literacy practice in a learning community of linguistically diverse learners. *Research in the Teaching of English,* 85–124.

Pearson, P. D., & Gallagher, M. C. (1983). The instruction of reading comprehension. *Contemporary Educational Psychology, 8*(3), 317–344.

Grammar and mechanics are integral to creating coherent and cohesive writing. Grammar is "the structural glue, the 'code' of language" (Purpura, 2004, p. IX). Grammar is not only the rules used to create well-formed sentences and the manipulation of clauses, phrases and other forms of syntax to create meaning but is also a resource for creating discourse that is *contextually*, situationally, and grammatically appropriate (Richards & Reppen, 2014). Students' use of *African-American Vernacular English* may be viewed by teachers as ungrammatical, but AAVE is based on syntactic rules that can be situationally appropriate (Linguistics Society of America, 2002). Mechanics refers to the technical aspects of writing that include spelling, punctuation, capitalization and use of abbreviations (Nordquist, 2020).

Knowledge of grammar and mechanics provides students with a fuller *understanding* of the communicative purposes of writing. "Students acquire knowledge and beliefs about how to write through mentoring, feedback, *collaboration*, and instruction" (Graham, 2019, pp. 286–287). Instruction that focuses on memorization of definitions, worksheets, and out-of-***context*** application results in little transfer to students' own writing (Hudson, 2016). In contrast, practices such as small-group sentence-combining activities that include student collaboration and active construction of knowledge can be effective for instruction in grammar and mechanics (Collet & Greiner, 2020). Using published authors' work as ***mentor texts*** can also increase knowledge of grammar (Ward, Collet, & Eilers, 2020). Knowledge of grammar and mechanics is utilized and enhanced through revision of writing, which requires critical thinking that considers the manipulation of content for clarity and meaning. [Contributed by Angelia C. Greiner & Vicki Stewart Collet]

Collet, V. S., & Greiner, A. C. (2020). Revisioning grammar instruction through collaborative lesson study. *Literacy Research & Instruction, 59*(2), 95–120.

Graham, S. (2019). Changing how writing is taught. *Review of Research in Education, 43*(1), 277–303.

Hudson, R. (2016). Grammar instruction. In C. A. MacArthur, S. Graham, & J. Fitzgerald (Eds.), *Handbook of writing research* (2nd ed., pp. 288–299). Guilford Press.

Linguistics Society of America. (2002). Resolution on the Oakland "Ebonics" issue. In L. Delpit & J. Kilgour Dowdy (Eds.), *The skin we speak: Thoughts on language and culture in the classroom* (pp. 223–224). The New Press.

Nordquist, R. (2020, July 19). *The mechanics of writing composition*. ThoughtCo. thoughtco.com/mechanics-composition-term-1691304

Purpura, J. E. (2004). *Assessing grammar*. Cambridge University Press.

Richards, J. C., & Reppen, R. (2014). Towards a pedagogy of grammar instruction. *RELC Journal, 45*(1), 5–25.

Ward, B., Collet, V. S., & Eilers, L. (2021). Using published authors as mentors to teach grammatical conventions. *Research Papers in Education*. Advance online publication.

Graphic organizers are a visual template for thinking often used in the preliminary stages of reading and writing. They aid *comprehension* and creative processes by providing a structured approach to *understanding,* brainstorming, and planning. Graphic organizers are also useful for activating *prior knowledge* (Merkley & Jefferies, 2001) in preparation for creating and reading texts and can easily be adapted for use across assignments and curriculums. Research has shown that graphic organizers improve comprehension for students at varying learning and language levels (Kim, 2004).

Teachers may use graphic organizers as a precursor to a larger assignment or as an ongoing companion to reading and writing assignments. The graphic organizer guides students as they work to plan or comprehend a text through note-taking. Graphic organizers can be especially helpful for language learners who are becoming familiar with and tracking *rhetorical moves* in texts (Vasquez & Coudin, 2018).

Examples of common graphic organizers include "*semantic* maps, semantic feature analysis, cognitive maps, story maps, framed outlines, and Venn diagrams" (Mede, 2010, p. 322). When creating and/or implementing graphic organizers, teachers should be careful not to construct organizers that are either too sparse or too detailed. An organizer that lacks sufficient structure could cause confusion or fail to provide adequate background information while an organizer that is too detailed could preclude a student from thoroughly reading the primary text (Merkley & Jefferies, 2001). An effective graphic organizer will ultimately gauge and activate students' prior knowledge, guide them in analysis and interpretation of a text, and serve as a visual guide for note-taking, planning, and tracking salient elements of a text. [Contributed by Megan Yates Grizzle]

Kim, A.-H., Vaughn, S., Wanzek, J., & Wie, S. (2004). Graphic organizers and their effects on the reading comprehension of students with LD: A synthesis of research. *Journal of Learning Disabilities, 37*(2), 105–118.

Mede, E. (2010). The effects of instruction of graphic organizers in terms of students' attitudes towards reading in English. *Procedia Social and Behavioral Science, 2,* 322–325.

Merkley, D. M., & Jefferies, D. (2001). Guidelines for implementing a graphic organizer. *The Reading Teacher, 54*(4), 350–357.

Vasquez, J. M. V., & Zuniga Coudin, R. (2018). Graphic organizers as a teaching strategy for improved comprehension of argumentative texts in English. *Revista Actualidades Investigatives en Educacion, 18*(2), 1–22.

Guided reading, a *differentiated instructional* method, promotes students' *literacy* skills through ***small-group instruction*** (Pinnell & Fountas, 2010). A system for active reading, guided reading often advances the essential components of reading—***phonemic awareness, phonics, fluency, vocabulary,*** and ***comprehension*** (Ellery, 2009)—with instructors explicitly leading students to strategies that enhance thinking and meaning-making.

In guided reading, teachers create small, *flexible groupings* of students with overlapping reading ability to promote dynamic literacy development (Pinnell & Fountas, 2010; Iaquinta, 2006). Teachers select leveled *fiction* and *nonfiction* books arranged by difficulty that challenge but do not frustrate students (Pinnell & Fountas, 2010). During small groups, instructors model pre-reading strategies to introduce the text before having students read silently or quietly. Teachers collect ***running records*** of *miscues* and monitor reading behaviors to assess student progress.

Guided reading allows *collaboration* between the teacher and students in the group. Through shared ***discussion*** and writing, students shape meanings of the text through their ability, experience, ***background knowledge,*** and emotions (Fountas & Pinell, 2012). By having students co-construct meaning through sharing of interpretations, teachers create value for the *multiple perspectives* within the group.

Explicitly teaching comprehension *strategies* expands student-driven meaning making of texts (Villaume & Brabham, 2001). Making predictions, *summarizing* key details, self-monitoring, or asking questions (Iaquinta, 2006) are all strategies that activate student awareness of independent reading skills. However, guided reading is only one part of ***comprehensive literacy instruction,*** which can include non-leveled book discussions, interactive ***read alouds,*** and self-selected ***independent reading*** (Fountas & Pinnell, 2012). [Contributed by Holly Sheppard Riesco] [See also Shared Reading/Writing]

Ellery, V. (2009). *Creating strategic readers: Techniques for developing competency in phonemic awareness, phonics, fluency, vocabulary, and comprehension.* International Reading Association.

Fountas, I. C., & Pinnell, G. S. (2012). Guided reading: The romance and the reality. *The Reading Teacher, 66*(4), 268–284.

Iaquinta, A. (2006). Guided reading: A research-based response to the challenges of early reading instruction. *Early Childhood Education Journal, 33*(6), 413–418.

Pinnell, G. S., & Fountas, I. C. (2010). Research base for guided reading as an instructional approach. In *Scholastic: Guided reading research.* Scholastic.

Villaume, S. K., & Brabham, E. G. (2001). Guided reading: Who is in the driver's seat? *The Reading Teacher, 55*(3), 260–263.

Independent reading/writing, put simply, is reading or writing that is done on one's own. In a classroom setting, this occurs as students engage independently in reading activities or produce their own writing by utilizing skills they were taught during previous guided practice (Davidson, 2007; Sanden, 2012).

In school settings, independent reading is often seen in the form of *silent reading* or *silent sustained reading* (SSR), a dedicated time for students to read silently in school. This has been found to increase reading ***motivation*** and enjoyment, especially when linked with student *choice* of reading material (Allred & Cena, 2020). Although by definition independent reading is done on one's own, Kelley and Clausen-Grace (2009) posit that teachers should provide simple structures and supports throughout the independent reading process—activities like *peer **discussion**,* student–teacher reading *conferences,* book talks, or reflective writings.

Literacy instruction, of course, requires ***modeling*** from the teacher, aimed at helping learners read and write in ways they previously couldn't on their own. Independent reading and writing, then, provides the opportunity to apply learned techniques and to show proficiency in reading and writing for a variety of *purposes* (Dorn et al., 1998). Although independent reading and writing are by definition done on one's own, Davidson (2007) argues that social learning is a valuable element, such as when student writers ask for and provide help to each other. In this sense, independent reading and writing are characterized by the teacher stepping back and allowing time for students to practice on their own, while still allowing for informal *peer-to-peer learning.* [Contributed by Johnny B. Allred] [See also Shared Reading/Writing; Guided Reading/Writing]

Allred, J. B., & Cena, M. E. (2020). Reading motivation in high school: Instructional shifts in student choice and class time. *Journal of Adolescent & Adult Literacy, 64*(1), 27–35.

Davidson, C. (2007). Independent writing in current approaches to writing instruction: What have we overlooked? *English Teaching: Practice and Critique, 6*(1), 11–24.

Dorn, L. J., French, C., & Jones, T. P. (1998). *Apprenticeship in literacy: Transitions across reading and writing.* Stenhouse.

Kelley, M. J., & Clausen-Grace, N. (2009). Facilitating engagement by differentiating independent reading. *The Reading Teacher, 63*(4), 313–318.

Sanden, S. (2012). Independent reading: Perspectives and practices of highly effective teachers. *The Reading Teacher, 66*(3), 222–231.

Informational texts, also known as *expository texts*, convey information about the natural or social world. Additionally, informational texts typically include technical ***vocabulary;*** classifications and definitions; *comparative/contrastive, problem/solution,* or *cause/effect* structures; recurring repetition of a main idea; and ***text features*** such as graphs, maps, indices, page numbers, and the like (Duke, 2003, p. 1). While informational texts can be written in a *narrative structure,* there are key features that differentiate *fictional **narrative texts*** from purely informational texts, most notably the temporal sequencing of events that is a definitive feature of narrative and is not inherent in exposition (Mantzicopoulos & Patrick, 2010, p. 414). Duke (2004) also argues that we read fictional narrative texts differently than we do informational texts, usually reading fictional narratives in their entirety and informational texts selectively for "just the parts that might meet our needs or interest us" (p. 3).

Research has demonstrated that reading informational texts can "facilitate the development of *content knowledge* and conceptual ***understanding*** as well as communicate processes of discipline-specific knowledge acquisition" (Mantzicopoulos & Patrick, 2010, p. 413). In this so-called Information Age, then, it is crucial that students learn to *critically read and write* about information. Even so, Duke found a striking scarcity of informational texts in classrooms, especially in elementary schools (2000). Because of this, she recommends four strategies for improving students' use of such texts: increased access to informational texts; increased time spent reading and discussing informational texts; explicitly teaching ***comprehension strategies***; and using informational texts for *authentic purposes* (2004, p. 2). When we incorporate more informational texts in the curriculum, we can spark students' curiosity while strengthening essential comprehension skills, "lay[ing] the groundwork for students to grow into confident, purposeful readers" (2004, p. 12). [Contributed by Kathryn Hackett-Hill] [See also Text Structures and Text Features]

Duke, N. K. (2000). 3.6 minutes per day: The scarcity of informational texts in first grade. *Reading Research Quarterly, 35*(2), 202–224.

Duke, N. K. (2003). Reading to learn from the very beginning: Information books in early childhood. *Young Children, 58*(2), 14–20.

Duke, N. K. (2004). The case for informational text. *Educational Leadership, 61*(6), 40–45.

Marntzicopoulos, P., & Patrick, H. (2010). "The seesaw is a machine that goes up and down": Young children's narrative responses to science-related informational text. *Early Education and Development, 21*(3), 412–444.

Integrated instruction combines English Language Arts with other discipline areas such as science, social studies, engineering, technology, and math. This *student-centered* method immerses learners in an approach to reading, writing, speaking, and listening that blurs the division of traditional subject areas. Integrated instruction enhances learners' conceptual understanding of real-world topics while simultaneously affirming the *reading-writing relationship*. Students make connections between subjects and competencies so that information, experiences, and skills can be applied to new learning situations in their complex world. This authentic approach leads to the development of *collaboration*, creativity, communication and *critical thinking* and problem solving as "...students become motivated to speak, write, discuss, and display their understanding to other students and adults" (Guthrie et al., 2000, p. 334).

In integrated instruction, a variety of **genres** from *fiction, nonfiction*, and primary and secondary sources are entwined with additional subject **standards**, permitting students to read and write across disciplines. Students explore through various lenses allowing for authentic *engagement* instead of isolated and segmented instruction. Integrated instruction provides an opportunity for students to combine ideas and experiences, resulting in an increase in **understanding**, retention, and application of concepts, as well as intrinsic reading **motivation**. Chen and colleagues (2013) describe an integrated fourth-grade writing and science experience in which, "...students were required to engage with connections among everyday language, scientific language, and audience language, rather than replicating scientific language for the teachers as often occurs in traditional classrooms" (p. 766). Carter and colleagues (2016) state, "The elementary classroom is uniquely designed to provide opportunities that integrate curriculum in meaningful ways," providing more depth and increased student engagement (p. 10). [Contributed by Leah R. Cheek] [See also Disciplinary Literacy]

Carter, V., Kindall, H., & Elsass, A. (2016). Integrating design and social studies: Engineering a play. *Children's Technology and Engineering, 20*(3), 10–13.

Chen, Y., Hand, B., & McDowell, L. (2013). The effects of writing-to-learn activities on elementary student's conceptual understanding: Learning about force and motion through writing to older peers. *Science Education, 97*(5), 745–771.

Guthrie, J., Wigfield, A., & VonSecker, C. (2000). Effect of integrated instruction on motivation and strategy use in reading. *Journal of Educational Psychology, 92*(2), 331–341.

Wilson-Lopez, A., & Gregory, S. (2015). Integrating literacy and engineering instruction for young learners. *The Reading Teacher, 69*(1), 25–33.

Intervention is targeted instruction offered in addition to classroom core instruction that gives attention to a student's identified needs based on *assessment* data, with the goal of improving the student's learning trajectory (Mesmer, 2008). Providing timely intervention can benefit a student immediately through the increase in quantity and quality of instruction. Students in all grades can benefit from targeted interventions (Fletcher & Vaughn, 2009; Scammacca, 2016).

The *Response to Intervention* (RtI) multitiered model is both an approach for early identification with intervention to reduce the number of students developing serious learning difficulties, as well as an approach to identifying students as learning disabled, an alternative approach to using the discrepancy between IQ and achievement model (Wixson, 2012).

The most popular of the RtI multitiered approaches is the three-tiered model. All students are screened, and those who do not pass undergo *progress monitoring*, which is frequent and quick assessments given to gauge the rate of learning and the effectiveness of the intervention (Fletcher, 2009; Mesmer, 2008). Tier I is the teacher's response to a student's needs within the core classroom instruction and is expected to address the needs of 80–85% of students (Wixson, 2012). The classroom teacher is responsible for gathering data, monitoring progress, and giving scientifically-based interventions in the least restrictive environment to any student in the classroom with learning struggles (Cassidy, 2016). Tier II is targeted *small-group instruction*, which is provided for students who did not make specified levels of progress in Tier I. Tier III is intensive intervention—including smaller groups, increased time in intervention, and/or intervention with a specialized teacher. Those students who do not make adequate progress in Tier III may be referred for an evaluation to determine eligibility for special education services. [Contributed by Wyann Stanton] [See also Small-Group Instruction]

Cassidy, J., Ortlieb, E., & Grote-Garcia, S. (2016). Beyond the common core: Examining 20 years of literacy priorities and their impact on struggling readers. *Literacy Research and Instruction*, 55(2), 91–104.

Fletcher, J. M., & Vaughn, S. (2009). Response to intervention: Preventing and remediating academic difficulties. *Child Development Perspectives*, 3(1), 30–37.

Mesmer, E. M., & Mesmer, H. A. E. (2008). Response to Intervention (RTI): What teachers of reading need to know. *The Reading Teacher*, 62(4), 280–290.

Scammacca, N. K., Roberts, G. J., Cho, E., Williams, K. J., Roberts, G., Vaughn, S. R., & Carroll, M. (2016). A century of progress: Reading interventions for students in grades 4–12, 1914–2014. *Review of Educational Research*, 86(3), 756–800.

Wixson, K. K., & Lipson, M. Y. (2012). Relations between the CCSS and RTI in literacy and language. *The Reading Teacher*, 65(6) 387–391.

Language development, the complex yet natural process of acquiring and sharing sounds, signs, and *symbols*, begins at birth. Its role is critical in that it helps us make sense of our world, share information, and create a foundation for thought. In trying to understand this process, along with all of its nuances, various theorists (e.g., Skinner, Chomsky, Piaget, *Vygotsky*) have offered insightful explanations. While each focused on different aspects, there are two concepts that have remained constant throughout: (a) individuals acquire language at different rates and (b) children's language development follows a series of stages (Clark, 2009).

With the brain's ability to discriminate and recognize sounds and rhythms, language development quickly moves from babbling, gestures, and word association to building meaningful ***vocabulary*** and assigning words to different categories such as verbs, nouns, and adjectives (Hoff, 2008). The toddler who was only using "book" to convey meaning quickly finds herself saying, "me book." As *oral language* continues to develop it builds upon everyday social interactions (e.g., listening, ***modeling,*** and mimicking), applying rules of *phonology,* ***morphology,*** *syntax,* ***semantics,*** and ***pragmatics*** along the way (Owens, 2016). In turn, this leads to an exponentially growing vocabulary, multi-word combinations, and finally, complete sentences such as, "Where is my book?" (Hoff, 2008).

At this point, *expressive language* skills (e.g., speaking, writing, or signing) continue to intertwine with *receptive language* skills (e.g., listening, reading, or seeing), and, over time, they build upon and into one another. The movement from *egocentric* or *private speech* (i.e., a child speaking aloud during play) to *inward speech* then sets the stage for the concrete to meet the abstract, and, in tandem, paves the way for *academic language.*

Understanding and applying language in the ***context*** of the classroom not only involves communicating ideas, information, and concepts in a particular content (Wright, 2015), but also fosters *critical thinking,* problem solving, and decision making. In sum, as we move through life, in or outside of the classroom, our environment will continue to influence and change our language. It will, however, always remain at the heart because after all, it is the tool we rely on to mediate our ideas, interactions, and relationships. [Contributed by Rebecca Carpenter de Cortina]

Clark, E. V. (2009). *First language acquisition.* Cambridge University Press.

Hoff, E. (2008). *Language development* (4th ed.). Wadsworth/Cengage Learning.

Owens, R. (2016). *Language development: An introduction* (9th ed.). Pearson.

Wright, W. E. (2015). *Foundations for teaching English language learners: Research, theory, policy, and practice* (2nd ed.). Caslon.

Learning progressions describe a ladder of skills and strategies that learners are expected to apply (Gallacher & Johnson, 2019). Ideally, learning progressions should be based on a set of *standards* that are scientifically and developmentally sound (Mosher & Heritage, 2017). The progression should move from concrete skills to abstract concepts; however, in *literacy* education, this process is difficult to describe because it is often not linear, as in science and mathematics (Gotwals & Songer, 2013; Mosher & Heritage, 2017). For example, literacy skills involving *genre* may develop in tandem with learning to *decode* print. Further, *comprehension strategies* may be practiced with the support of a model reader who reads the text aloud, eliminating the *decoding* barrier.

Learning progressions can be helpful in planning instruction and for monitoring students' progress toward an element of a standard (Bailey & Heritage, 2014). For example, a broad standard might mention textual analysis, which suggests that in order to meet this standard, the student might need to be a fluent reader with good *comprehension* as well as genre knowledge. In this case, requisite knowledge is essential for student success. While a set of content standards may be developmentally and discipline appropriate, in order to develop sound learning progressions, the standards must be examined for their component parts (Gallacher & Johnson, 2019; Mosher & Heritage, 2017).

When learning progressions are well developed, they allow for *individualized instruction* that addresses a variety of student needs (Bailey & Heritage, 2014; Mosher & Heritage, 2017). Learning progressions should be flexible enough to accommodate the learning of students who excel and those who require extra practice or *intervention* (Bailey & Heritage, 2014; Gallacher & Johnson, 2019; Mosher & Heritage, 2017). [Contributed by Judy L. Fields]

Bailey, A. L., & Heritage, M. (2014). The role of language learning progressions in improved instruction and assessment of English language learners. *Tesol Quarterly, 48*(3), 480–506.

Gallacher, T., & Johnson, M. (2019). "Learning progressions": A historical and theoretical. *Education, 26*(1), 21–51.

Gotwals, A. W., & Songer, N. B. (2013). Validity evidence for learning progression-based assessment items that fuse core disciplinary ideas and science practices. *Journal of Research in Science Teaching, 50*(5), 597–626.

Mosher, F., & Heritage, M. (2017). *A hitchhiker's guide to thinking about literacy, learning progressions, and instruction.* CPRE Research Reports.

Literacy, traditionally described as reading and writing, has been expanded to include different and multiple *literacies.* Literacy is the construction of meaning from variously composed forms of text. It is the ability to identify, understand, interpret, create, and communicate using visual, audible, and digital materials across disciplines and sociocultural contexts (Scribner, 1984; Street, 1995). This broad definition recognizes the multiple modes and contexts in which literate practices occur.

Functionalist definitions of literacy emphasize development of skills necessary for participation in society and may narrowly equate literacy with technical skills such as **decoding, fluency,** and *spelling.* More broadly, literacy has been described as a means for fulfilling individual aspirations. Through literacy, people acquire, construct, and communicate meaning. Literacy is the sea on which ideas flow among people and places.

Literacy is a complex practice, nested in and sustained by social and cultural activity (Brandt, 2001). The image of an isolated scholar pouring over a book of necessity includes those involved in writing, publishing, and distributing that text, as well as all those whose ideas contributed, over time and across space, to the meanings included in the text being perused. Literacy emerges from a social milieu. It is not an individual accomplishment.

Literacy is a valuable commodity, connected with hope and heartache, exploration and exploitation. Literacy involves intellectual and *aesthetic* participation with accumulated knowledge available through multiple means and modes. Literacy may maintain hegemony and political powerlessness; it may also be a resource for social transformation (Freire, 1970; Scribner, 1984).

Literacy's expansive scope and meaning recognize and call for a diversity of community- and school-based approaches to literacy learning. Effective means for acquisition of literacy are responsive to needs for functional skills, social power, and self-improvement (Scribner, 1984). Although the description of literacy provided here is intentionally broad and shadowy, any definition of literacy is arguable, and the meaning and methods of literacy are not static. "There can be neither a first nor a last meaning," as individuals, cultures, and societies create "ever new ways to mean" (Bakhtin, 1981, pp. 345–346). [Contributed by Vicki Stewart Collet] [See also New Literacies]

Bakhtin, M. M. (1981). *The dialogic imagination.* University of Austin Press.

Brandt, D. (2001). *Literacy in American lives.* Cambridge University Press.

Freire, P. (1970). *Cultural action for freedom* (Mon. Series no. 1). Harvard Educational Review.

Scribner, S. (1984). Literacy in three metaphors. *American Journal of Education, 93*(1), 6–21.

Street, B. V. (1995). *Social literacies: Critical perspectives on literacy in development, ethnography and education.* Longman.

Literary devices are techniques that writers use to artfully convey meaning or create a specific effect. Working with elements of literature like character and plot, literary devices are purposefully utilized to deepen the meaning of a work or heighten the emotional and aesthetic quality of the writing, producing a text that is pleasurable, evocative, or meaningful for readers. (While a writer or speaker may use a literary device as a *rhetorical device* or factor to persuade an audience, the primary purpose of a literary device is to enrich literary works.)

Common literary devices include imagery, motif, allusion, symbol, irony, alliteration, and more. Other prevalent literary devices include types of *figurative language*, or nonliteral language, like metaphor, simile, hyperbole, understatement, and idiom. Figurative language is often employed in writing and speech to clarify thinking (Roberts & Kreuz, 1994, p. 161) that typically reflects a certain cultural model (Lakoff & Johnson, 2011). Newkirk (2014) adds that figurative expression, most notably metaphor, is useful because it translates "something new and complex into more manageable scenarios...link[ing] the new to the known" (p. 64). Likewise, writers often compare abstract concepts to concrete objects to ground readers in ideas that may otherwise be inconceivable. In "Hope is the Thing with Feathers," for instance, Dickinson compares hope to a bird–an animal that connotes freedom, vitality, and resilience–to conjure a vivid image that enables readers to comprehend an abstract concept. While an idea like hope can certainly be defined in more literal or technical terms, a writer, like Dickinson, may utilize a literary device to explain an idea in a fresher, more memorable, or more powerful way than conventional language.

Corden (2007) found that it can be beneficial to draw students' attention to literary devices by prompting them to read as writers and notice how these tools shape a works' meaning and emotional resonance. By doing so, he concludes that "a critical evaluation of literature and an examination of literary devices can help children become more reflective writers" and critical readers (p. 29). [Contributed by Kathryn Hackett-Hill] [See also Rhetorical Factors and Devices]

Corden, R. (2007). Developing reading-writing connections: The impact of explicit instruction of literary devices on the quality of children's narrative writing. *Journal of Research in Childhood Education, 21*(3), 269–289.

Dickinson, E. (2019). *Hope is the thing with feathers.* Oxford University Press.

Lakoff, G., & Johnson, M. (2011). Metaphors we live by. In J. O'Brien (Ed.), *The production of reality: Essays and readings on social interactions* (5th ed., pp. 124–134). Sage.

Newkirk, T. (2014). *Minds made for stories: How we really read and write informational and persuasive texts.* Heinemann.

Roberts, R. M., & Kreuz, R. J. (1994). Why do people use figurative language? *Psychological Science, 5*(3), 159–163.

Mentor texts, also called *model texts,* are books, articles, or other text selections, usually from published sources, that are used during writing instruction to provide models for writing. Research suggests that reading, discussing, and evaluating mentor texts can have a positive impact on the quality of students' *independent writing* (Corden, 2007; Snyders, 2014).

Mentor texts can be enabling or constraining, depending on teachers' management of the lesson (Myhill et al., 2018). When instruction has a clear learning focus and connects choices to authorial intentions, students are more likely to incorporate these intentional choices (in varying ways and to differing degrees), rather than simply imitating the mentor text. If the teaching focus is too strongly directed to the text itself, rather than authorial intent, the mentor text may be constraining, leading to limited learning about writing.

When students notice and name the author's techniques, they may develop increased conceptual knowledge of language craft and how it can be manipulated (Zuideman, 2012). Effective use of mentor texts may also include revising or editing snippets of the author's work. As teachers and students discuss authors' use of writing features, they can conjecture why the authors made these writerly moves and consider how to use such constructions in their own writing. Through **discussion** of authors' **motivation** for their writing choices, students may become more aware of the active role that writers play as they construct their texts, including making choices about **semantics,** *syntax,* and **literary devices** (Ward et al., 2021).

Mentor texts provide opportunities for contextualized instruction in all **genres** and may provide aspirational models for students' writing. Using published authors as mentors for students' writing provides authentic models for students to construct knowledge about writing within meaningful contexts. (Mentor texts are distinguished from *anchor texts,* which are examples of different levels of student writing used to illustrate *rubrics.*) [Contributed by Vicki Stewart Collet]

Corden, R. (2007). Developing reading-writing connections: The impact of explicit instruction of literary devices on the quality of children's narrative writing. *Journal of Research in Childhood Education, 21*(3), 269–289.

Myhill, D., Lines, H., & Jones, S. (2018). Texts that teach: Examining the efficacy of using texts as models. *L1 Educational Studies in Language and Literature, 18,* 1–24.
https://doi.org/10.17239/L1ESLL-2018.18.03.07

Ward, B., Collet, V., & Eilers, L. (2021). Using published authors as mentors to teach grammatical conventions. In *Research papers in education.* Advance online publication.

Zuidema, L. A. (2012). The grammar workshop: Systematic language study in reading and writing contexts. *English Journal, 101*(5), 63–71.

Miscue analysis is a way of ***understanding*** students' reading skill by examining where *oral reading* does not match the printed text. The approach is founded on the idea that the reading process is made up of interrelated skills that work together to produce skilled reading. *Miscues* may be associated with one of three **cueing systems:** *graphophonic* (letter-sound correspondence), *syntactic* (sentence structure), and **semantic** (meaning). By assigning errors to a specific *cueing system*, teachers can target instruction to support skills and strategies that result in more *fluent reading* (Allen & Watson, 1976; Goodman, 1969).

Miscue analysis requires an oral reading sample coded by the teacher; a ***running record*** could be used for this analysis. *Error rates* (total words/total errors), *accuracy* rates (total words read—total errors/total words), and *self-correction* rates (number of errors + number of self-corrections/number of self-corrections) maybe be calculated; self-correction is viewed as evidence that readers are attending to cueing systems.

Retrospective miscue analysis is a variation of miscue analysis which draws the child into *dialogue* with the teacher about miscue patterns (Goodman et al., 1996). The teacher preselects miscues that are impacting reading and thinks through strategies to support the reader.

Miscue analysis has been criticized because miscues account for only a small portion of words that are read (Ehri, 2020) and because it does not focus enough on skilled word reading (Wixson, 1979). However, others support it; for example, Hoffman and colleagues (2020) describe the value of this practice for supporting responsive teaching, and Noguerón-Liu (2020) suggests miscue analyses can increase ***understanding*** of how *emerging bilinguals* draw from their multiple language and ***literacy*** resources. [Contributed by Savanna L. Gragg] [See also Cueing Systems]

Allen, P. D., & Watson, D. J. (1976). *Findings of research in miscue analysis: Classroom implications.* National Council of Teachers of English.

Ehri, L. C. (2020). The science of learning to read words: A case for systematic phonics instruction. *Reading Research Quarterly, 55,* S45–S60.

Goodman, K. (1969). Analysis of oral reading miscues: Applied psycholinguistics. *Reading Research Quarterly, 5*(1), 9–30.

Goodman, Y. M. (1996). Revaluing readers while readers revalue themselves: Retrospective miscue analysis. *Reading Teacher, 49*(8), 600–609.

Noguerón-Liu, S. (2020). Expanding the knowledge base in literacy instruction and assessment: Biliteracy and translanguaging perspectives from families, communities, and classrooms. *Reading Research Quarterly, 55,* S307–S318.

Wixson, K. L. (1979). Miscue analysis: A critical review. *Journal of Reading Behavior, 11*(2), 163–175.

Modeling is a strategy or tool a person can use to demonstrate a task, skill, or process so that the observer(s) internalizes the task, skill, or process being modeled. Historically, modeling included *comprehension,* word solving, and *text structures and features* (Fisher & Frey, 2015). From a *literacy* viewpoint, both reading and *writing processes* can be modeled; however, a teacher can model in any content area. A *think aloud,* where a teacher verbalizes their thought processes, is a modeling activity.

Modeling provides students the skills to analyze and access complex text (Fisher & Frey, 2015). Schutz & Rainey (2017) consider a categorization of three interrelated parts of modeling: showing, situating, and abstracting. Showing is making the thinking and doing work evident to students. Situating is drawing connections to previous/current learning (content or practice). Abstracting helps learners transfer a process or skill to another task.

Students can also engage in modeling. Students could think aloud with a partner to model their thoughts when reading a text or they could attempt to emulate the skill the teacher previously demonstrated. A teacher may use *a gradual release of responsibility* with modeling a skill as student learning occurs (Santa, 2006).

Student achievement and teacher awareness increase when teachers model their thinking (Fisher, Frey, & Lapp, 2011). Modeling through demonstrating processes that are a part of the content also increases student comprehension (Santa, 2006). Modeling is an essential component of a teachers' practice. "Research suggests that explicit teacher demonstration and modeling is imperative for effective literacy learning" (Frey et al., 2005, p. 279). [Contributed by Afton Schleiff] [See also Think Aloud; Gradual Release of Responsibility]

Fisher, D., & Frey, N. (2015). Teacher modeling using complex informational texts. *The Reading Teacher, 69*(1), 63–69.

Fisher, D., Frey, N., & Lapp, D. (2011). Coaching middle-level teachers to think aloud improves comprehension instruction and students reading achievement. *The Teacher Educator, 46*(3), 231–243.

Frey, B., Lee, S., Tollefson, N., Pass, L., & Massengill, D. (2005). Balanced literacy in an urban school district. *The Journal of Educational Research, 98*(5), 272–280.

Santa, C. (2006). A vision for adolescent literacy: Ours or theirs? *Journal of Adolescent & Adult Literacy, 49*(6), 466–476.

Schutz, K. M., & Rainey, E. C. (2017). Making sense of modeling in elementary literacy instruction. *The Reading Teacher, 73*(4), 443–451.

Morphology is the study of word formation, specifically the parts of words that have meaning (Lieber, 2015). The term was originally coined in the nineteenth century as a biological term by German philosopher Johann Wolfgang von Goethe; its Greek etymology, *morph-*, literally means "shape, form" (Aronoff & Fudeman, 2011). As it relates to *literacy/ies,* morphology is helpful in guiding readers in the construction and deconstruction of words within the target language being studied.

Morpheme. This is the smallest meaningful linguistic unit within a word—smallest because it cannot be divided into smaller meaningful elements, and meaningful because it contains a grammatical function (Aronoff & Fudeman, 2011; International Literacy Association, n.d.).

Free Morpheme. Some morphemes can stand alone as words (e.g., cat, chair, lamp). These are considered "free" in that they do not need other morphemes to form a word.

Bound Morpheme. In contrast to free morphemes, these cannot stand alone as words by themselves (e.g., *-s*, *-ly*, *-ed*). While they possess meaning, they must be attached to other morphemes to form a word.

Root. This term, along with "stem" and "base" (see below), is used to refer to the part of a word that remains when all affixes (see below) have been removed; it cannot be broken down into smaller elements morphologically (Bauer, 1983). For instance, the word "astronomy" contains two morphemes: astro- and -nomy; "astro" is the root.

Base. This *free morpheme* gives the word its basic meaning and is sometimes also a root. Base words can have affixes (see below) added at their beginning or end to change the word's meaning or part of speech. However, "base" and "root" cannot always be used interchangeably. For example, in the word "unbreakable," "breakable" could be considered the base for prefixation to create "unbreakable," but "breakable" would not be referred to as the root because it can be broken down into smaller meaningful parts morphologically.

Affix. This refers to a *syllable* or letter combination added to the beginning of a word (i.e., prefix) or the end of a word (i.e., suffix) to change its meaning or part of speech. [Contributed by Seth D. French]

Aronoff, M., & Fudeman, K. (2011). *What is morphology?* (Vol. 8). John Wiley & Sons.

Bauer, L. (1983). *English word-formation.* Cambridge University Press.

International Literacy Association. (n.d.). *Literacy glossary.*
    https://literacyworldwide.org/get-resources/literacy-glossary

Lieber, R. (2015). *Introducing morphology.* Cambridge University Press.

Motivation, in a *literacy* context, is a term that describes a learner's desire to participate and engage in literacy activities. Motivation drives behavior: if students are motivated to read, they will spend more time reading, exert higher cognitive effort during reading, and be more committed to comprehending what they are reading. In turn, these students will become more competent and confident in their literacy abilities, increasing their motivation to read or write even more (Guthrie & Wigfield, 2000).

Learners are motivated for a host of different reasons, but psychological research organizes motivation factors into two categories: intrinsic and extrinsic (Deci & Ryan, 1985). In a literacy context, learners who are intrinsically motivated will read or write because they are genuinely interested in doing so; the process brings excitement or enjoyment (Guthrie & Wigfield, 2000). Extrinsic motivation, on the other hand, is characterized by a focus on external incentives or recognition, or to avoid punishment.

Research has explored instructional strategies that increase intrinsic motivation for literacy activities. One approach is to offer students *choice* in what or how they read or write (Allred & Cena, 2020; Miller & Anderson, 2009). Another approach is to find topics and texts that build upon students' ***background knowledge*** or personal interests and to *design* literacy activities around those texts (Becker et al., 2010). A third strategy is to identify texts or activities that provide a moderate challenge to the learner—difficult enough that it helps them develop and grow as a literacy learner, but not so challenging that they get frustrated from repeated failure or struggle (Turner, 1995). As teachers and literacy specialists identify and implement methods for increased motivation in reading and writing, learners will be more *engaged* and will develop literacy skills more rapidly and authentically. [Contributed by Johnny B. Allred]

Allred, J. B., & Cena, M. E. (2020). Reading motivation in high school: Instructional shifts in student choice and class time. *Journal of Adolescent & Adult Literacy, 64*(1), 27–35.

Becker, M., McElvany, N., & Kortenbruck, M. (2010). Intrinsic and extrinsic reading motivation as predictors of reading literacy: A longitudinal study. *Journal of Educational Psychology, 102*(4), 773–785.

Deci, E. L., & Ryan, R. M. (1985). *Intrinsic motivation and self-determination in human behavior.* Plenum.

Guthrie, J. T., & Wigfield, A. (2000). Engagement and motivation in reading. In M. L. Kamil, P. B. Mosenthal, P. D. Pearson, & R. Barr (Eds.), *Handbook of reading research* (Vol. 3, pp. 403–422). Routledge.

Miller, D., & Anderson, J. (2009). *The book whisperer: Awakening the inner reader in every child.* Jossey-Bass.

Turner, J. C. (1995). The influence of classroom contexts on young children's motivation for literacy. *Reading Research Quarterly, 30*(3), 410–441.

Multicultural literature is literature that is created by or focused on under-represented groups. Multicultural literature includes books, poems and other forms of writing that provide readers with the opportunity to validate their sense of self, connect with the world around them, and support their access to academic language and literacies (Morrell, 2012). Quality multicultural texts provide authentic depictions of the beliefs, experiences, and *perspectives* of less-dominant groups that in turn allow students to 'read with and against' the narratives they encounter (Morrell, 2012). While authors who are members of the group depicted generally offer such authenticity, non-members can offer such legitimacy as well (Brown, 2021).

The use of multicultural texts serves as "mirrors, windows, and sliding glass doors" (Bishop, 1990) for students, allowing readers to see themselves reflected in the text as well as providing an opportunity to explore the lives and perspectives of people that are unfamiliar. Furthermore, multicultural texts allow students to grapple with multiple perspectives on multiple topics.

Historically, there has been a lack of multicultural children's literature in comparison to children's literature that features White main characters (Bold, 2018). In recent years, multicultural literature has grown to encompass much more than textual representations of people of color to include differences in gender, sexual orientation, and disabilities (Yokota, 2001). Literature that reflects and represents underrepresented groups extends the traditional, Western canon to reflect a more pluralistic society, aiding in student *engagement* and self-empowerment (López-Robertson & Haney, 2017). This broader view of multicultural texts considers issues of oppression, opposition, and marginalization within society, fostering empathy and *understanding* of others. The use of multicultural texts is also an essential component of *culturally responsive instruction.* [Contributed by Angelia C. Greiner]

Bishop, R. S. (1990). Mirrors, windows, and sliding glass doors. *Perspectives: Choosing and Using Books for the Classroom, 6*(3), ix–xi.

Bold, M. R. (2018). The eight percent problem: Authors of color in the British young adult market (2006–2016). *Publishing Research Quarterly, 34,* 385–406.

Brown, B. (2021, February). *A guide to selecting multicultural literature: Separating the wheat from the chaff.* Boston University.

López-Robertson, J., & Haney, M. (2017). Their eyes sparkled: Building classroom community through multicultural literature. *Journal of Children's Literature, 43*(1), 48–54.

Morrell, E. (2012). Multicultural readings of multicultural literature and the promotion of social awareness in ELA classrooms. *New England Reading Association Journal, 47*(2), 10–16.

Yokota, J. (2001). *Kaleidoscope: A multicultural booklist for grades K-8* (3rd ed.). National Council of Teachers of English.

Multimodality refers to the use of multiple modes to communicate; a *mode* is simply a means of communication (International Literacy Association, n.d.). Language, sounds, *symbols*, pictures, diagrams, graphics, and videos are all examples of modes that can be used to communicate a message. When any combination of these or other modes is used to create meaning, we refer to this as multimodality. The term is closely tied to theories rooted in linguistics, including systemic functional linguistics, social semiotic theory, and conversation analysis (Jewitt, 2017).

In our current digital age, it could perhaps go without saying that "language is no longer the carrier of all meaning" as it may have been at one point in time (Kress, 2000, p. 339). Rather, multimodality so permeates the world we live in that we could argue it is "the normal state of human communication" (Kress, 2010, p. 1). This is because different modes offer unique affordances to make their message more clear, engaging, and accessible to *diverse audiences*. As new *digital technologies* are created and made more available to growing numbers of people, the ability to create and consume multimodally is in some ways what it means to be literate by today's standards.

Consequently, teachers in today's classrooms who exclusively use the written word to engage their students and create assignments that exclusively focus on students' ability to compose the written word must seriously evaluate the extent to which their classrooms are preparing students to effectively navigate life outside the classroom; instead, engaging students in producing and responding to video, videogames, comics, graphic novels, textiles, and other diverse modes must become common practice (Rowsell, 2013). Students today need ample opportunities to compose and interact multimodally, both for the sake of facilitating their engagement with classroom content and equipping them to effectively engage with the increasingly multimodal world we live in. [Contributed by Seth D. French] [See also Digital Literacies; New Literacies]

International Literacy Association. (n.d.). *Literacy glossary.*
    https://literacyworldwide.org/get-resources/literacy-glossary
Jewitt, C. (2017). Multimodal discourses across the curriculum. In S. L. Thorne & S. May (Eds.), *Language, education, and technology* (3rd ed., pp. 31–43). Springer.
Kress, G. (2000). Multimodality: Challenges to thinking about language. *TESOL Quarterly, 34*(2), 337–340.
Kress, G. R. (2010). *Multimodality: A social semiotic approach to contemporary communication.* Taylor & Francis.
Rowsell, J. (2013). *Working with multimodality: Rethinking literacy in a digital age.* Routledge.

A **narrative text,** or story, is a mode of writing in which events within a time frame are artfully ordered in a pattern of tension and resolution, *cause and effect.* This order of events, also known as the *plot,* generates drama and momentum in the story, propelling the *characters* forward in an escalating series of conflicts toward a final resolution. Peter Elbow describes it as "a well-planned *sequence* of yearnings and reliefs, itches and scratches" (2011, p. 303). Narrative texts can be either *fictional* or *nonfictional;* however, not all ***informational texts*** are structured as narratives.

The traditional narrative structure, emulating an arc, rises and falls as the story progresses and includes an exposition that introduces the characters, *setting,* and *conflict* of the story; a period of *rising action* in which the conflict accelerates for the main character; a *climax,* or crisis, in which the tension of the story reaches its peak, resulting in the main character's turning point; a period of *falling action* that explores the consequences of the climax; and a *denouement* in which the conflict is usually resolved (Jago et al., 2011). (Jago and colleagues also note that some narratives diverge from this structure, and it can be a worthwhile exercise to examine when, how, and why they do.) Similarly, the events in a story may be sequenced *chronologically,* though writers may employ plot devices like foreshadowing and flashbacks or begin in medias res to create a narrative that is out of chronological order. Research suggests that when students are aware of these ***story grammars,*** or typical narrative ***text structures,*** they will have fewer problems comprehending narrative texts (Dymock & Nicholson, 1999).

Likewise, reading and writing narrative texts are central to comprehending our lives and our world because "narrative imagining—story—is the fundamental instrument of thought. It is our chief means of looking into the future, of predicting, of planning, or explaining" (Turner, 1996, pp. 4–5). John S. O'Connor refers to this as making "story-sense" of the senseless in our lives (2011, p. 14). Perhaps, then, in reading and writing narrative texts, it is possible to impose order and compose ourselves to illuminate ***understanding.*** [Contributed by Kathryn Hackett-Hill]

Dymock, S. J., & Nicholson, T. (1999). *Reading comprehension: What is it? How do you teach it?* New Zealand Council for Educational Research.

Elbow, P. (2011). *Vernacular eloquence: What speech can bring to writing.* Oxford University Press.

Jago, C., Shea, R. H., Scanlon, L., & Aufses, R. D. (2011). *Literature & composition: Reading, writing, thinking.* Bedford/St. Martin's.

O'Connor, J. S. (2011). *This time it's personal: Teaching academic writing through creative nonfiction.* National Council of Teachers of English.

Turner, M. (1996). *The literary mind.* Oxford University Press.

New literacies as a term carries different meanings in different contexts; it can refer to newly emerging social practices of *literacy,* new proficiencies needed to effectively navigate online/digital spaces, or new discourses of communication. Rather than see these differences as sources of contention, it's more appropriate to view them as sources of *collaborative* theory development. So, new literacies theory can be conceptualized on two levels: lowercase (new literacies) and uppercase (**New Literacies**) (Leu et al., 2015).

Lowercase theories deal with specific areas of new literacies and new technologies, such as the social transactions that occur within platforms like TikTok or Snapchat. Consequently, these theories are better equipped for keeping pace with the ongoing changes occurring in these diverse literacy spaces. The broader theory of New Literacies is a more inclusive concept that contains the findings shared across diverse lowercase theories (Leu et al., 2015). Donald J. Leu and colleagues (2015) outline the following eight principles shared among these lowercase lines of research in new literacies:

1. The Internet is this generation's defining technology for literacy and learning within our global community.
2. The Internet and the other technologies require New Literacies to fully access their potential.
3. New Literacies are deictic (Coiro et al., 2008).
4. New social practices are a central element of New Literacies.
5. New Literacies are multiple, multimodal, and multifaceted, and, as a result, our ***understanding*** of them benefits from multiple points of view.
6. Critical literacies are central to New Literacies.
7. New forms of strategic knowledge are required with New Literacies.
8. Teachers become more important, though their role changes, in new literacy classrooms.

New literacies are "new" because change is constant within the social, economic, cultural, intellectual, and institutional spaces we inhabit (ILA, n.d.). As a result, new literacies must be regularly integrated, assessed, and embodied in today's classrooms. [Contributed by Seth D. French] [See also Digital Literacies; Multimodality; Literacy/Literacies]

Coiro, J., Knobel, M., Lankshear, C., & Leu, D. J. (2008). Central issues in new literacies and new literacies research. In C. Lankshear, M. Knobel, J. Coiro, & D. J. Leu (Eds.), *Handbook of research on new literacies* (pp. 1–21). Taylor & Francis.

International Literacy Association. (n.d.). *Literacy glossary.* https://literacyworldwide.org/get-resources/literacy-glossary

Leu, D. J., Slomp, D., Zawilinski, L., & Corrigan, J. A. (2015). Writing research through a New Literacies lens. In C. A. MacArthur, S. Graham, & J. Fitzgerald (Eds.), *Handbook of writing research* (2nd ed., pp. 41–56). The Guilford Press.

Peer response is defined by Liu and Hansen (2002) as the "use of learners as sources of information, and interactants for each other in such a way that learners assume roles and responsibilities normally taken on by a formally trained teacher, tutor, or editor..." (p. 1) such that students learn from each other as they respond and critique both each other's writing through oral or written feedback. Peer response, also referred to as *peer review* or *peer editing*, encompasses more than simple editing of the *mechanics* of student writing by providing an opportunity for students to interact with their peers' writing on a more comprehensive level, commenting on *rhetorical issues*, content creation and the extension of ideas.

Peer response is supported by constructivist and *sociocultural theories* in that through peer interaction "the process of negotiation and construction of shared meaning" is emphasized (Roselli, 2016, p. 261). Utilizing peer response in the classroom promotes student dialogue that fosters thinking and develops reasoning skills (Vygotsky, 1978). Peer response has also been shown to be an effective strategy in writing instruction for *emergent bilinguals* (Liu & Hansen, 2002).

Although peer response is most often associated with writing instruction, peer response can be utilized in other classroom activities as well. Training students to provide "reader-based," constructive feedback rather than evaluative, judgmental feedback ensures a productive, supportive environment (Elbow, 1998). In addition, "think-aloud" peer feedback can be particularly effective with adolescent writers. (Beck, 2018). Regardless of form, at the heart of peer response is substantive *collaboration* among peers. Computer-mediated interaction through online *discussion* threads and chat spaces can also serve to promote synergistic peer responses (Staarman, Krol, & van der Meijden, 2005). [Contributed by Angelia C. Greiner]

Beck, S. W. (2018). *A think-aloud approach to writing assessment: Analyzing process & product with adolescent writers.* Teachers College Press.

Davenport, M. (2016, September 22). *Socratic seminars: Building a culture of student-led discussion.* Edutopia. https://www.edutopia.org/blog/socratic-seminars-culture-student-led-discussion-mary-davenport

Elbow, P. (1998). *Writing with power.* Oxford University Press.

Liu, J., & Hansen, J. (2002). *Peer response in second language writing classrooms.* University of Michigan Press.

Roselli, N. D. (2016). Collaborative learning: Theoretical foundations and applicable strategies to university. *Propósitos y Representaciones, 4*(1), 219–280.

Staarman, J. K., Krol, K., & van der Meijden, H. (2005). Peer interaction in three collaborative learning environments. *Journal of Classroom Interaction, 40*(1), 29–39.

Vygotsky, L. S. (1978). *Mind in society: The development of higher psychological processes.* Harvard University Press.

Perspective and **point of view** are sometimes used interchangeably, but it is important to note there is a distinct difference. Perspective is shaped by a person's thoughts, values, feelings, and actions (Al-Alami, 2019; Rasley, 2008). It focuses on how the narrator or *characters* are telling the *story* or event while drawing on the reader or listener's **background knowledge** and lived experiences to process what is happening.

For example, a five-year old's perspective of *The Giving Tree* will most likely be very different than his mother's. While the child may see generosity, his mom might see self-sacrifice. Another example would be how a group of teachers experience Lesson Study. Although they observed the same lesson, each of them will see and contribute something unique to the learning cycle. Responses to a text or an event will most often be seen differently, and what is shared will depend on who is being asked and how it is told.

Point of view (POV), on the other hand, is the *voice* of the person who is telling the story or event (Wyile, 1999). It uses aspects of perception such as sense as well as thoughts and emotions to underline and shape the **narrative** (Rasley, 2008; Wyile, 1999). POV allows writers to vicariously interact with readers and provide a vehicle to travel through the story (Rasley, 2008).

When conveying a message or telling a story, authors can choose four different narrative *stances* (Wyile, 1999): (a) *first person,* when the message or events are being told through the eyes of a character; (b) *second person,* when the narrator is speaking to the reader directly; or (c) *third person omniscient or limited,* when the narrator acts as a spectator to tell a story or event. What is interesting, and oftentimes surprising, is when an author alternates or shifts from one POV to another (Rasley, 2008). In sum, "POV is reader-oriented but author controlled" (Rasley, 2008, p. 6).

It is critical that students are exposed to multiple perspectives and have many opportunities to practice recognizing and applying different POVs. Increasing, this knowledge will not only expand their **comprehension,** analytical, and problem-solving skills, but also give them a greater sense of empathy. In turn, it is hoped they would further develop their appreciation for how stories and events are told as well as who is telling them. [Contributed by Rebecca Carpenter de Cortina]

Al-Alami, S. (2019). Point of view in narrative. *Theory and Practice in Language Studies, 9*(8), 911–916.

Rasley, A. (2008). *The power of point of view: Make your story come to life.* Writer's Digest Books.

Silverstein, S. (1964). *The giving tree.* HarperCollins.

Wyile, A. S. (1999). Expanding the view of first-person narration. *Children's Literature in Education, 30,* 185–202.

Phonics is the relationship between sounds (*phonemes*) and their visual counterparts (*graphemes*) in both transparent and opaque orthographies (Johnston, McGeown, & Watson, 2012). In *transparent orthographies*, phonetic relationships are predictable and stable; in *opaque orthographies*, such as English, phonetic relationships are sometimes irregular (Johnston, McGeown, & Watson, 2012). For example, the phoneme /ī/ is represented by more than one *orthographic pattern* in words such as "like," "sight," "fly," and "bye." However, the phoneme /ĭ/ is more stable in words such as "big" and "lick."

Phonetic and graphemic relationships may be taught through both *synthetic* and analytic phonics instruction (Ehri, 2020; Johnston, McGeown, & Watson, 2012). Both approaches address word-solving skills and strategies based on orthographic patterns (Johnston, McGeown, & Watson, 2012; Scanlon & Anderson, 2020). The goal of both approaches is to support reading **comprehension** and *written expression* (Scanlon & Anderson, 2020). Ideally, instruction in either approach—or a combination thereof—includes explicit **modeling**, systematic review, and application for mastery of both **decoding** and *encoding* knowledge (Scanlon & Anderson. 2020). Either approach may be informed by *developmentally appropriate instruction*. For example, *Ehri's model* of reading describes four *developmental phases of reading*: 1) pre-*alphabetic*, 2) *partial-alphabetic*, 3) *full-alphabetic*, and 4) *consolidated-alphabetic* (Ehri, 2020). Henderson and Templeton (1986) describe five developmental stages of *spelling* competence: 1) pre-literate, 2) letter name, 3) within word, 4) *syllable* juncture, and 5) derivational relations. It should be noted that reading phases and developmental spelling stages are not intended to be regarded as linear progressions. For example, a learner may exhibit characteristics of more than one phase of reading or stage of spelling simultaneously.

Analytic phonics is a meaning-based approach that prompts attention to words and/or units of sound, their orthographic counterparts, and the **context** in which they occur (Johnston, McGeown, & Watson, 2012; Scanlon & Anderson, 2020). For example, comprehension is facilitated through the application of word-solving strategies. Interpretation of orthographic patterns may be derived through analogy and/or sound units such as syllables, *onset/rime*, blends, digraphs, *vowel* sounds, and *consonant* clusters (Johnston et al., 2012).

Synthetic phonics is a skills-based approach in which individual phonemes and graphemes are explicitly taught and practiced using *decodable texts* and phoneme-grapheme (*orthographic*) *mapping* (Ehri, 2020). The goal of this approach is to promote *automaticity* and *accuracy* in both decoding and *encoding* to support *comprehension* and *written expression*.

When decoding and encoding words, the *segmenting* and *blending* of sounds is common. After isolating individual sounds, each may then be associated with spelling patterns. For example, to decode the word "red," a reader might segment the sounds in the word (/r/ /ĕ/ /d/). The reader then blends the sounds into a word unit. To check for meaning, the reader must understand that "red" is a color and not the past tense of "read" (/r/ /ē/ /d/). This holds true for encoding as well. The writer must choose the correct spelling pattern to convey intended meaning. Segmenting and blending can present problems when sound units are not clearly defined and articulated (Ehri, 2020; Scanlon & Anderson, 2020). *Decodable texts* may be used for practice of phoneme-grapheme relationships, but it is also critical for students to practice decoding of rich texts so that sounds and visual properties of words are stored in memory along with their meaning (Ehri, 2020).

Although some evidence suggests *systematic phonics instruction* may not be superior to other approaches (Bowers, 2020), it does incorporate explicit instruction and a developmentally appropriate scope and *sequence* which "… provides foundational knowledge that launches students' development" (Ehri, 2020, p. s55). [Contributed by Judy L. Fields]

Bowers, J. S. (2020). Reconsidering the evidence that systematic phonics is more effective than alternative methods of reading instruction. *Educational Psychology Review, 32,* 681–705.

Ehri, L. C. (2020). The science of learning to read words: A case for systematic phonics instruction. *Reading Research Quarterly, 55,* S45–S60.

Henderson, E. H., & Templeton, S. (1986). A developmental perspective of formal spelling instruction through alphabet, pattern, and meaning. *The Elementary School Journal, 86*(3), 305–316.

Johnston, R. S., McGeown, S., & Watson, J. E. (2012). Long-term effects of synthetic versus analytic phonics teaching on the reading and spelling ability of 10 year old boys and girls. *Reading and Writing, 25*(6), 1365–1384.

Scanlon, D. M., & Anderson, K. L. (2020). Using context as an assist in word solving: The contributions of 25 years of research on the Interactive Strategies Approach. *Reading Research Quarterly, 55,* S19–S34.

Phonological and phonemic awareness are terms referring to knowledge children have about the sound systems of language. Phonological awareness is a broad term that refers to the ability to understand the sound system at several levels: words, *syllables, onset* and *rime, rhymes, and alliterations*. Phonological awareness includes phonemic awareness. Phonemic awareness is a narrow term referring to knowledge of *phonemes* (the smallest sounds of the language). These skills include isolation, blending, segmenting and manipulations. This distinction is often illustrated with an umbrella labelled phonological awareness and water droplets for each skill listed above including phonemic awareness and its associated skills. Research has associated phonological knowledge with increased skills in reading and *spelling* (Bradley & Bryant, 1983). Anthony and Francis (2005) explain that phonological awareness is critical to reading, develops in a predictable pattern, and should be taught systematically with other *literacy* skills.

Teaching Phonological Awareness. There are many strategies for teaching phonological awareness; all are based in *oral language* exchanges. Activities might include clapping for each word in a sentence, counting syllables in multisyllabic words, and matching words that have the same first sound or rhyming endings. These activities are oral because they are focused on hearing the sounds and rhythms of words.

Teaching Phonemic Awareness is also primarily an oral activity that may include pictures of words but does not include written words and letters. A teacher working on *phoneme isolation* might ask a child, "What is the first sound you hear when you say cat?" *Blending* and *segmentation* are opposite skills. In a blending activity the teacher will stretch out a word, saying each phoneme and asking the child to blend the sounds together and say the word. Conversely, in a segmenting activity, the teacher would say the word, then ask the student to stretch the word and say individual sounds. Phonemic manipulations are practiced by adding sounds to words, deleting sounds from words, and substituting sounds. [Contributed by Savanna L. Gragg]

Anthony, J. L., & Francis, D. J. (2005). Development of phonological awareness. *Current Directions in Psychological Sciences, 14*(5), 255–259.

Bradley, L., & Bryant, P. E. (1983). Categorizing sounds and learning to read—a causal connection. *Nature Publishing Group, 301*(3), 419–421.

Pragmatic knowledge is implicit or explicit *understanding* of the functions or *purposes* of language, how it is used and impacts speakers' *points of view*, the choices they make, and the constraints they face in social interactions (Crystal, 2008). Pragmatic knowledge is closely related and complementary to *semantic knowledge,* which involves word meanings. Some linguists argue that the nature of language cannot be fully understood without studying pragmatics (Leech, 2014).

Pragmatics speaks to the notion that meaning is not static and depends on the *context* of the *setting*, social situations, communication *styles*, *background knowledge*, types of *discourse*, and cultural conventions, among other factors (Goddard, 1998; Owens, 2016). For example, how students discuss a writing assignment and ask the teacher questions in class differs from when they informally talk about a meme at lunch in the cafeteria. Both involve discourse, but pragmatics shape each situation differently.

Aspects surrounding pragmatics are vast in nature and include: (a) *implicature*, information used by a speaker to make the connection of what was actually said and what was meant; (b) *presuppositions*, propositions of what the speaker implicitly assumes to be known by the listener; (c) *reference*, a speaker's use of one linguistic expression to help the listener access *prior knowledge* and interpret the other; (d) *deixis*, forms in language referring to properties of expressions where meaning is constant but shifts due to changes in referents; (e) *speech acts*, direct or indirect actions such as requests, questions, commands or statements that involve interpersonal relations; and (f) *(in)definiteness*, issues associated with noun phrases and their uniqueness, familiarity, strength or specificity (Horn & Ward, 2004).

In sum, pragmatics plays an important role in and outside of the classroom. Through experience and interactions, pragmatic knowledge not only helps students develop communication skills such as initiating and ending conversations, turn taking, expressing *opinions*, and agreeing or disagreeing (Wright, 2015), but also reflects their multiple *identities* and everyday real world experiences. [Contributed by Rebecca Carpenter de Cortina]

Crystal, D. (2008). *Language library: A dictionary of linguistics and phonetics* (6th ed.). Wiley.

Goddard, C. (1998). *Semantic analysis: A practical introduction.* Oxford University Press.

Horn, L. R., & Ward, G. (Eds.). (2004). *The handbook of pragmatics.* Blackwell.

Leech, G. N. (2014). *Principles of pragmatics.* Routledge.

Owens, R. (2016). *Language development: An introduction* (9th ed.). Pearson.

Wright, W. E. (2015). *Foundations for teaching English language learners: Research, theory, policy, and practice* (2nd ed.). Caslon.

Question Answer Relationships (QAR) are question types, based on the Pearson and Johnson (1978) question taxonomy, that provide a framework for teachers and students to cultivate and answer *comprehension* questions (Raphael, 1986). There are two main categories of questions: in-the-book or text-dependent questions and in-the-reader's-mind or knowledge-based questions. In-the-book questions can be refined further to "Right There" and "Think and Search" or "Putting it Together" (Raphael, 1986). The answer to a "Right There" question is a detail from the text that can be found in one sentence (Raphael, 1986; Raphael 1982). "Think and Search" answers have to be pieced together by the reader using various parts of the text. Questions categorized as "in the reader's mind" can also be segmented into two types: "Author and You" and "On My Own" (Raphael, 1986). Distinguishing between the two types depends on whether or not the text has to be read for the reader to answer the question. If it does, then it is an "Author and You" question, and if it does not, it is an "On My Own" question, drawing from the reader's *background knowledge* (Raphael, 1986).

QAR can be a useful tool for teachers to ask effective questions at various parts of a text (Raphael, 1986). To extend learning, teachers could draw primarily on "On My Own" or "Author and You" QARs (Raphael, 1986). "As a tool for students, QAR instruction can provide the basis for three *comprehension strategies*: (1) locating information, (2) **determining** *text structures* and how these structures may convey information, and (3) determining when an inference would be required or invited" (Raphael, 1986, p. 521). QAR can also provide a common language for teachers and students (Raphael & Au, 2005).

Research has shown that students of all ages benefit from QAR instruction; students make inferences and comprehend text using information from the reading and from their background knowledge (Raphael, 1986). Teachers of younger students may begin QAR instruction by introducing the two main categories and adding in the distinctions as students develop an *understanding*. [Contributed by Afton Schleiff] [See also Assessment; Comprehension]

Raphael, T. (1982). Question-answering strategies for children. *The Reading Teacher, 36*(2), 186–190.

Raphael, T. (1986). Teaching question answer relationships, revisited. *The Reading Teacher, 39*(6), 516–522.

Raphael, T. E., & Au, K. H. (2005). QAR: Enhancing comprehension and test taking across grades and content areas. *The Reading Teacher, 59*(3), 206–221.

Read alouds include a teacher or designated reader *orally* reading a text, usually to a group and for instructional purposes. Read alouds are among the most commonly reported memories of elementary classroom experiences (Fisher, Flood, Lapp & Frey, 2004). These experiences often involve books that students could not read successfully on their own, but when they experience the book as a group, they are able to engage with the *vocabulary,* discuss *story elements* and *text features,* and make connections between the book and their own experiences. Lane and Wright (2007) identified three primary strategies teachers use during read alouds: *dialogic reading* (focuses on active child participation, *modeling* more sophisticated language, and creating a challenging conversation), *text talk* (focuses on a few target vocabulary words and deep *discussion* of those words through the text), and *print referencing* (focuses on text features and forms of print and engages students in *discussions* to increase interest in reading). When planning, teachers should consider three phases of the read-aloud experience: before reading, during reading, and follow up. Teachers' actions in each part of the read aloud will impact students' ability to actively participate with the text.

Common features of read alouds were identified by Fisher, Flood, Lapp and Frey (2004): (1)intentional book selection; (2) teachers practiced reading the selected text; (3) the book was purposefully connected with the lesson and the learning objective was shared with students; (4) teachers read *fluently* and modeled *prosody*, specifically, using animation and emotion as they read; (5) teachers paused reading and engaged with listeners during the story; and (6) teachers linked the experience *to independent reading and writing* practices. Effective read alouds encourage *language development,* increase vocabulary depth and breadth, promote independent interest in reading, and engage students in meaningful *dialogue* (Beck & Mckeown, 2001). [Contributed by Savanna L. Gragg]

Beck, I. L., & Mckeown, M. G. (2001). Text talk: Capturing the benefits of read-aloud experiences for young children. *The Reading Teacher, 55*(1), 10–20.

Fisher, D., Flood, J., Lapp, D., & Frey, N. (2004). Interactive read-alouds: Is there a common set of implementation practices? *The Reading Teacher, 58*(1), 8–17.

Lane, H. B., & Wright, T. L. (2007). Maximizing the effectiveness of reading aloud. *The Reading Teacher, 60*(7), 668–675.

Readability calculates the ease or difficulty in *comprehending* text, often by applying a readability formula. The purpose of determining readability is to assist classroom teachers in choosing books which will ultimately help their students become better readers. Fry (2002) clarifies that readability formulas, "…usually give a numerical score to rank books or other reading matter in order of difficulty…" which can result in a corresponding grade level suggestion. Factors such as *word choice,* sentence length, *syllable* count, and *text complexity* are analyzed, typically using computer software, and the results are published in forms such as *Lexile,* **Guided Reading,** or DRA *levels.* The readability level of a text can be a benchmark that assists teachers in selecting grade-level appropriate readings for their students. "Selecting books by a readability formula or leveling procedure is only one of the many teaching techniques that a reading teacher should use, but it is one that will help many students have a successful learning experience" (Fry, 2002).

As readers develop and mature, text selection requires multilayered decisions based on *text complexity.* "The concept of text complexity is based on the premise that students become stronger readers by reading increasingly challenging texts" (Grant et al., 2015). Text complexity challenges students to use **comprehension strategies** to synthesize their **background knowledge** with the information from the text as they are exposed to new ways of thinking and new knowledge. Text complexity is determined quantitatively, qualitatively, and by analyzing the needs of the individual reader. Quantitative text complexity is measured numerically using the before-mentioned readability formulas. There are more than one hundred readability formulas in existence (Fry, 2002). Qualitative text analysis necessitates content exploration by a teacher who considers **text structure**, author's *purpose,* and **literacy** *devices* such as writing *style* and **vocabulary.** Qualitative decisions can be guided by scoring *rubrics* providing visual support for evaluation. Ultimately, however, readability analysis may be trumped by students' reading goals, interests, and background knowledge for teacher- or student-selected texts. [Contributed by Leah R. Cheek]

Fry, E. (1968). A readability formula that saves time. *Journal of Reading, 11*(7), 513–578.

Fry, E. (2002). Readability versus leveling. *The Reading Teacher, 56*(3), 286–291.

Grant, M., Moss, B., & Lapp, D. (2015). *A close look at close reading: Teaching students to analyze complex texts, grades K-5.* ASCD.

Reading Recovery is a 16–20 week, one-on-one *intervention* that accelerates *literacy* achievement of students who appear to be behind after their first year of schooling. Daily lessons by a Reading Recovery-trained teacher include 1) reading and rereading of easy texts, including *discussion* of *miscues*; 2) composing and reading messages or stories; 3) activities for analyzing words; and 4) reading new texts with support (Pinnell et al., 1994).

Marie Clay (1991), who developed Reading Recovery based on evidence from systematic observation of young readers, found that children used ***phonological***, *orthographic*, *syntactic*, and ***semantic*** resources (***cueing systems***) to negotiate texts in ways that became increasingly robust and agile over time. Reading Recovery lessons may include activities such as clapping *syllables*, *Elkonin boxes*, manipulating letters, writing letters on multiple surfaces, and attending to spelling patterns. There is no predetermined *sequence* for learning skills; rather, specific activities are based on need. One study (Iversen & Tunmer, 1993) found that additional ***phonics*** instruction increased the effectiveness of Reading Recovery lessons.

Although some studies of Reading Recovery have been critiqued, a preponderance of evidence demonstrates its effectiveness when compared with other one-on-one approaches, similar approaches with *small groups*, and similar interventions with shorter teacher training (D'Agostino & Harmey, 2016; Pinnell et al., 1994; What Works Clearinghouse, 2008).

Reading Recovery and Teacher Learning. In Reading Recovery, teacher development is a key to accelerating young readers' progress. A year-long intensive preparation program includes regular behind-the-glass opportunities to observe Reading Recovery lessons followed by facilitated reflection, "*Collaborative* discussions focused on individual students support the development of responsive teaching" (Compton-Lily et al., 2020, p. S191). [Contributed by Vicki Stewart Collet]

Clay, M. M. (1991). *Becoming literate: The construction of inner control.* Heinemann.

Compton-Lilly, C. F., Mitra, A., Guay, M., & Spence, L. K. (2020). A confluence of complexity: Intersections among reading theory, neuroscience, and observations of young readers. *Reading Research Quarterly, 55*, S185–S195.

D'Agostino, J. V., & Harmey, S. J. (2016). An international meta-analysis of reading recovery. *Journal of Education for Students Placed at Risk (JESPAR), 21*(1), 29–46.

Iversen, S., & Tunmer, W. E. (1993). Phonological processing skill and the reading recovery program. *Journal of Educational Psychology, 85*(1), 112–126.

Pinnell, G. S., Lyons, C. A., & DeFord, D. E. (1994). Comparing instructional models for the literacy education of high-risk first graders. *Reading Research Quarterly, 29*(1), 8–39.

What Works Clearinghouse. (2008, December). *Reading Recovery*® [WWC intervention report]. Institute of Education Sciences. https://readingrecovery.org/wp-content/uploads/2016/12/wwc_reading_recovery_report_08.pdf

Reading-writing relationships are a linked association suggesting skilled reading leads to competent writing and writing leads to improved reading. The reading-writing relationship is generally associated with one of three theoretical models focusing on either cognitive, socio-cognitive, or combined reading and *writing processes* (Shanahan, 2016). From a cognitive approach, reading and writing share four foundational constructs: *background knowledge,* metaknowledge, *text structures,* and procedural knowledge. A socio-cognitive approach focuses on the underlying foundation of both reading and writing, communication. The third model combines the processes inherent to only writing and inherent to only reading so that when combined they solve a problem or reach a goal, such as *content learning.*

Recent cognitive research suggests that reading-to-write instructional models may be superior to writing-to-read models, and that the relationship between reading and writing is strongest at the word level, lessening over time as the complexity of language learning increases (Ahmed et al., 2014). Within socio-cognitive studies, *audience awareness* and *peer response* have been shown to improve *persuasive* and *argumentative writing* for older students (Moore & McArthur, 2012). From the perspective of combining reading and writing to accomplish a goal, Graham and Hebert (2010) found that student *comprehension* of new information improved when students wrote about what they had read.

NCTE's (2016) policy statement on teaching writing notes writing and reading are related, students engaged in reading frequently find writing easier, and writing may help students in reading by emphasizing *phonemic awareness* and *phonics knowledge.* In turn, reading contributes to background knowledge, audience awareness, and *text structures* for writing. [Contributed by Angelia C. Greiner]

Ahmed, Y., Wagner, R. K., & Lopez, D. (2014). Developmental relations between reading and writing at the word, sentence, and text levels: A latent change score analysis. *Journal of Educational Psychology, 106,* 419–434.

Graham, S., & Hébert, M. (2011). Writing to read: A meta-analysis of the impact of writing and writing Instruction on reading. *Harvard Educational Review, 81,* 710–744.

Moore, N. S., & MacArthur, C. A. (2012). The effects of being a reader and of observing readers on fifth grade students' argumentative writing and revising. *Reading and Writing, 25,* 1449–1478.

National Council Teachers of English. (2016, February 28). *Professional knowledge for the teaching of writing.* https://ncte.org/statement/teaching-writing/

Shanahan, T. (2016). Relationships between reading and writing development. In C. MacArthur, S. Graham, & J. Fitzgerald (Eds.), *Handbook of writing research* (2nd ed., pp. 194–207). Routledge.

Reciprocal teaching is an instructional approach to improve student reading *comprehension.* Reciprocal teaching is a form of "guided practice in applying simple, concrete strategies to the task of text comprehension" (Brown & Palincsar, 1989, p. 413). The use of reciprocal teaching involves explicitly teaching students four reading strategies through teacher *guided practice* with the idea that students gradually master the use of these techniques in their own self-monitoring of text comprehension. The four reading strategies include: generating questions about the text, *summarizing* information, clarifying word meanings and confusing text, and predicting what will happen next in a text (Rosenshine & Meister, 1994).

In reciprocal teaching, teachers first *model* the four *comprehension strategies* in a section of text, then students are asked to read the next section of text using the strategies in a *dialogue* format with the teacher. As the reading progresses, students eventually take on more of the responsibility of continuing the dialogue with the four reading strategies within reading groups or with a partner. The four comprehension strategies were coined the "Fab Four" by Oczkus (2005) to increase student *engagement* and help students remember each strategy, personifying each strategy as a character with props (Predicting Paul, Clarifying Clarabelle, Questioning Queen, Summarizing Sam) that could be adopted by both teachers and students to internalize the techniques.

A key part of reciprocal teaching is the ***discussion*** that generates from the students' use of questions designed to elicit student predicting, summarizing, clarifying and questioning of the text. Reciprocal teaching is an appropriate technique for use with *fiction* as well as *nonfiction* texts at any grade level (Stricklin, 2011). [Contributed by Angelia C. Greiner][See also Comprehension Strategies]

Brown, A. L., & Palincsar, A. S. (1989). Guided, cooperative learning and individual knowledge acquisition. In L. B. Resnick (Ed.), *Knowing, learning and instruction: Essays in honor of Robert Glaser* (pp. 393–451). Erlbaum.

Oczkus, L. D. (2005). *Reciprocal teaching strategies at work: Improving reading comprehension, grades 2–6.* International Reading Association.

Rosenshine, B., & Meister, C. (1994). Reciprocal teaching: A review of the research. *Review of Educational Research, 64*(4), 479–530.

Stricklin, K. (2011). Hands on reciprocal teaching: A comprehension technique. *The Reading Teacher, 64*(8), 620–625.

Rhetorical factors and devices are the choices an author or speaker makes in order to convey meaning and purpose to an intended *audience*. More specifically, rhetorical factors refer to outside influences, such as audience and intent, while rhetorical devices refer to the techniques an author or speaker ultimately employs.

Before crafting a speech or written text, an author will first analyze audience and purpose (Demirdogen, 2010). In order to effectively reach an intended audience, a speaker or writer must consider elements such as the audience's culture and community, the medium in which the text or speech is presented, the audience's familiarity with the given topic, and any biases the audience may have. The speaker or writer should also anticipate or be aware of the audience's reactions to a text. Unlike the fixed elements of *grammar,* rhetorical factors are fluid, changing as a writer or speaker uses and manipulates language to reach an intended audience (Braverman, 2013). It may also be worthwhile to examine ways in which the author's *identity* relates to the audience. "There are ways in which we spontaneously, intuitively, and unconsciously persuade ourselves" (Burke, 1966), and those factors affect how a speaker or writer gains audience identification. A speaker or writer cannot effectively use rhetorical devices without considered these rhetorical factors.

Rhetorical devices are moves a speaker or writer makes in order to reach an audience and achieve a specific effect. Rhetorical devices are essentially a speaker or writer's toolbox, a place from which the most effective means of communication are chosen. Rhetorical devices can range from linguistic stylistic choices such as tone, diction, and syntax to *genre* such as persuasive, informative, and argumentative. Rhetorical appeals fall under the umbrella of rhetorical devices. Ethos, logos, and pathos, commonly referred to as the Rhetorical Triangle, are the three rhetorical appeals identified by Aristotle. Writers and speakers can use rhetorical appeals to inform or persuade an audience. It is important for writers and speakers to be aware of the working relationship between ethos, logos, and pathos and use them "intentionally and judiciously" (Varpio, 2018) as they seek to persuade or inform an audience. [Contributed by Megan Yates Grizzle] [See also Literary Devices]

Braverman, C. (2015). *A rhetoric of literate action: Literate action, Volume I.* WAC Clearinghouse.

Burke, K. (1966). *Language as symbolic action.* University of California Press.

Demirdogen, U. D. (2010). The roots of research in (political) persuasion. *International Journal of Social Inquiry, 3*(1), 189–201.

Varpio, L. (2018). Using rhetorical appeals to credibility, logic, and emotions to increase your persuasiveness. *Perspectives on Medical Education, 7*(3), 207–210.

Running records are an *assessment* tool used to track students' reading as they read aloud. Clay (1993) developed the running record as an observation tool to identify reading difficulties. To conduct a running record, a teacher and student use copies of the same text as the student reads aloud and the teacher codes each word (correct, omitted, inserted, substituted, repeated, *self-corrected* and so on) (Clay, 2000). The assessment is brief (1–3 minutes) and should be conducted frequently. Using running records allows the teacher to see results of *interventions* and skill growth as the student applies them to reading. Running records allow teachers to track changes in *accuracy* and may also be used to track changes in rate. Aside from tracking individual learner progress, a teacher can also use running records to quickly identify misconceptions or skill needs in the whole classroom. This information could be used to strategically form *small group instruction* and mini lessons. Research supports instructional decision-making processes that are closely connected to student assessments, and running records are one way teachers can employ "precision teaching" as Fountas and Pinnell (2012, p. 276) call it. Running records can move *guided reading* from a leveled-reader teaching focus to a skill teaching focus, moving learners along the continuum of reading more smoothly. Running records allow for a deeper look at the inaccuracies of student reading when analyzed using *miscue analysis.* Since running records do not measure *comprehension,* they should be used as part of a *comprehensive literacy assessment* plan. [Contributed by Savanna L. Gragg]

Clay, M. M. (1993). *An observation survey of early literacy achievement.* Heinemann.

Clay, M. M. (2000). *Running records: For classroom teachers.* Heinemann.

Fountas, I. C., & Pinnell, G. S. (2012). Guided reading the romance and the reality. *The Reading Teacher, 66*(4), 268–284.

Scaffolding is a form of assistance that enables a novice to solve a problem, carry out a task, or achieve a goal which would otherwise be beyond his ability. However, the focus is not on merely completing the task. Instead, scaffolding results in a better ***understanding*** on the part of the learner of how to conceptualize and accomplish the task (Collet, 2015). That is, a genuine change in understanding has occurred, not merely some end state (e.g., a correctly edited sentence).

Unlike our everyday notion of scaffolding during building construction, in which the same apparatus would be needed each time one set out to construct a similar building, in *instructional scaffolding*, over time less and less scaffolding would be needed to accomplish the same task because the learner's ability has increased.

Scaffolding is associated with Vygotsky's (1978) concept of **the *zone of proximal development*,** which includes tasks that a learner can do only with assistance. However, the term *scaffolding* was first used by Bruner (Wood, Bruner, & Ross, 1976) when describing language acquisition. Scaffolding helps learners to cope with the complexity of tasks authentically by keeping the task whole while helping learners to understand and manage the parts (Clark & Graves, 2005). Wells (1999) lists three features of educational scaffolding: 1) the dialogic nature of the *discourse* in which knowledge is co-constructed; 2) the significance of the kind of activity in which knowing is embedded, and 3) the role of artifacts that mediate knowing.

In a classroom, the teacher might *differentiate* by giving everyone the same task, but by providing varying types of scaffolding. For example, before reading, one student (or group of students) might be introduced to key ***vocabulary*** and strategies for determining their meaning. Another might have sticky notes that say "Stop & Think" placed at various spots in the text. The purpose of these scaffolds would be to build students' internal strategies for reading so that in the future they could use these skills more independently. Scaffolds provided by the teacher are intended to increase the learner's ability; however, teachers' ability to scaffold may be limited by their own predetermined frames or knowledge. [Contributed by Vicki Stewart Collet]

Collet, V. S. (2015). The gradual increase of responsibility model for coaching teachers: Scaffolds for change. *International Journal of Mentoring and Coaching in Education, 4*(4), 269–292.

Clark, K., & Graves, M. (2004). Scaffolding students' comprehension of text. *The Reading Teacher, 58*(6), 570–580.

Vygotsky, L. S. (1978). *Mind in society: The development of higher psychological processes.* Harvard University Press.

Wood, D. J., Bruner, J., & Ross, G. (1976). The role of tutoring in problem solving. *Journal of Child Psychology and Psychiatry, 17,* 89–100.

Science of reading, broadly defined, is research results from a variety of fields and methodologies, including basic and applied science, related to reading and reading instruction. The science of reading is supported by ongoing research with a "dynamic interplay among methods, theories, and findings" (Pearson, 2020). Examining this full range of science "can be a helpful policy guide to initiatives that seek to improve students' reading ability and appetite" (Collet et al., 2021).

The current scientific body of knowledge about reading, including implementation science, demonstrates the importance of *oral language* skills, ***phonological awareness,*** and letter knowledge (Cervetti et al., 2020; Ehri, 2020; Melby-Lervåg et al., 2012), the value of ***decoding*** skills in early reading and how the influence of such skills attenuates over time (Ehri, 2020; Garcia & Cain, 2014), how ***sight words*** support ***comprehension*** (Ehri, 2020), the critical role of *content knowledge* in comprehending texts (Cabell & Hwang, 2020; Cervetti & Wright, 2020), benefits of instruction in ***phonics, fluency, comprehension strategies,*** and ***text structure*** (Afflerbach et al., 2020; Ehri, 2020; Pyle et al., 2017; Rasinski et al., 2009), the interconnection between reading and writing (Graham, 2020), the benefits of extended ***discussion*** (Elizabeth et al., 2012; Heath, 2013), the influence of social and cultural *contexts* (Bloome, 1985; Heath, 2013) and ***motivation*** and *engagement* (Guthrie & Klauda, 2014; Taylor et al., 2003) in ***literacy*** learning and practice, that comprehension at all levels is supported by ***semantic*** and *embodied* processes and influenced by the reader's *cultural knowledge* (Compton-Lily et al., 2020; Orellana, 2015), that learning to read is a long-*term developmental process* (Cervetti et al., 2020), that effective reading instruction is complex (Hindman et al., 2020) and much more. Because of the complexity of reading and the differences among learners and contexts, no single instructional approach has been found to be effective in teaching all students to read (Compton-Lily et al., 2020; International Dyslexia Association, 2018; Malloy et al., 2019).

Some instantiations of the "science of reading" are narrowly construed to emphasize basic research from cognitive psychology, neuroscience, and linguistics that describe how the brain learns to read in the early years. Public discourse sometimes focuses on the alphabet principle (Liberman et al., 1989) and a ***simple view of reading*** (Gough & Tunmer, 1986). This overly-restrictive view "is being used to shape public policy and silence other ***perspectives***" (Hoffman et al., 2020, p. S258) and to narrow curricula (Compton-Lily et al., 2020; Vaughn et al., 2020) and should not be confused with the body of scientific studies of reading, which includes an interdisciplinary store of knowledge about "reading-related skills, processes, antecedents, and outcomes" (Alexander, 2020, p. S90). A "cautionary disposition to avoid drawing unwarranted inferences about the efficacy of pedagogical alternatives that have not themselves been rigorously examined" (Cervetti et al., 2020, p. S168) is needed. In contrast, research on reading instruction and the preparation of *literacy* teachers is robust, extensive, and useful for guiding reform efforts (Hoffman et al., 2020).

The science of reading involves how reading "operates, develops, is taught, shapes academic and cognitive growth, affects *motivation* and emotion, interacts with context, and impacts *context* in turn" (Graham, 2020, p. S35). It includes genetic, biological, neurological, cognitive, linguistic, psychological, environmental, contextual, social, political, historical, and cultural factors that influence the acquisition and use of reading (Alexander et al., 2020; Graham, 2020). It is "the scientific study of all facets of reading, including its consequences for readers and society as a whole" (Graham, 2020, p. S35). At times controversial, the science of reading is an ongoing body of research, "an area for inquiry rather than a foregone conclusion" (Woulfin et al., 2020, p. S111). [Contributed by Vicki Stewart Collet]

Afflerbach, P., Hurt, M., & Cho, B.-Y. (2020). Reading comprehension strategy instruction. In D. L. Dinsmore, L. K. Fryer, & M. M. Parkinson (Eds.), *Handbook of strategies and strategic processing* (pp. 98–118). Routledge.

Alexander, P. A. (2020). What research has revealed about readers' struggles with comprehension in the digital age: Moving beyond the phonics versus whole language debate. *Reading Research Quarterly, 55*, S89–S97.

Bloome, D. (1985). Reading as a social process. *Language Arts, 62*(2), 134–142.

Cabell, S. Q., & Hwang, H. (2020). Building content knowledge to boost comprehension in the primary grades. *Reading Research Quarterly, 55*, S99–S107.

Cervetti, G. N., Pearson, P. D., Palincsar, A. S., Afflerbach, P., Kendeou, P., Biancarosa, G., Higgs, J. Fitzgerald, M., & Berman, A. I. (2020). How the reading for understanding initiative's research complicates the simple view of reading invoked in the science of reading. *Reading Research Quarterly, 55*, S161–S172.

Cervetti, G. N., & Wright, T. S. (2020). The role of knowledge in understanding and learning from text. In E. B. Moje, P. Afflerbach, P. Enciso, & N. K. Leseaux (Eds.), *Handbook of reading research* (Vol. 5, pp. 237–260). Routledge.

Collet, V. S., Penaflorida, J., French, S., Allred, J., Greiner, A., & Chen, J. (2021). Red flags, red herrings, and common ground: An expert study in response to state reading policy. *Educational Considerations.*

Compton-Lilly, C. F., Mitra, A., Guay, M., & Spence, L. K. (2020). A confluence of complexity: Intersections among reading theory, neuroscience, and observations of young readers. *Reading Research Quarterly, 55*, S185–S195.

Ehri, L. C. (2020). The science of learning to read words: A case for systematic phonics instruction. *Reading Research Quarterly, 55*, S45–S60.

Elizabeth, T., Ross Anderson, T. L., Snow, E. H., & Selman, R. L. (2012). Academic discussions: An analysis of instructional discourse and an argument for an integrative assessment framework. *American Educational Research Journal, 49*(6), 1214–1250.

García, J. R., & Cain, K. (2014). Decoding and reading comprehension: A meta-analysis to identify which reader and assessment characteristics influence the strength of the relationship in English. *Review of Educational Research, 84*(1), 74–111.

Gough, P. B., & Tunmer, W. E. (1986). Decoding, reading, and reading disability. *Remedial and Special Education, 7*(1), 6–10.

Graham, S. (2020). The sciences of reading and writing must become more fully integrated. *Reading Research Quarterly, 55*, S35–S44.

Guthrie, J. T., & Klauda, S. L. (2014). Effects of classroom practices on reading comprehension, engagement, and motivations for adolescents. *Reading Research Quarterly, 49*(4), 387–416.

Heath, S. B. (2013). It's a book! It's a bookstore! Theories of reading in the worlds of childhood and adolescence. In D. E. Alvermann, N. J. Unrau, & R. B. Ruddell, (Eds.), *Theoretical models and processes of reading* (6th ed., pp. 204–227). International Reading Association.

Hindman, A. H., Morrison, F. J., Connor, C. M., & Connor, J. A. (2020). Bringing the science of reading to preservice elementary teachers: Tools that bridge research and practice. *Reading Research Quarterly, 55*, S197–S206.

Hoffman, J. V., Hikida, M., & Sailors, M. (2020). Contesting science that silences: Amplifying equity, agency, and design research in literacy teacher preparation. *Reading Research Quarterly, 55*, S255–S266.

International Dyslexia Association. (2018). *Knowledge and practice standards for teachers of reading* (Rev. ed.). Author.

Liberman, I. Y., Shankweiler, D., & Liberman, A. M. (1989). *The alphabetic principle and learning to read.* University of Michigan Press.

Melby-Lervåg, M., Lyster, S. A., & Hulme, C. (2012). Phonological skills and their role in learning to read: A meta-analytic review. *Psychological Bulletin, 138*, 322–352.

Orellana, M. F. (2015). *Immigrant children in transcultural spaces: Language, learning, and love.* Routledge.

Pearson, P. S. (2020, September). *Making sense of the science of reading.* International Literacy Association Intensive. https://ila.digitellinc.com/ila/live/83/page/447?timezone=America/Chicago

Pyle, N., Vasquez, A. C., Lignugaris/Kraft, B., Gillam, S. L., Reutzel, D. R., Olszewski, A., ... Pyle, D. (2017). Effects of expository text structure interventions on comprehension: A meta-analysis. *Reading Research Quarterly, 52*(4), 469–501.

Rasinski, T., Rikli, A., & Johnston, S. (2009). Reading fluency: More than automaticity? More than a concern for the primary grades? *Literacy Research and Instruction, 48*(4), 350–361.

Taylor, B. M., Pearson, P. D., Peterson, D. S., & Rodriguez, M. C. (2003). Reading growth in high-poverty classrooms: The influence of teacher practices that encourage cognitive engagement in literacy learning. *The Elementary School Journal, 104*(1), 3–28.

Vaughn, M., Parsons, S. A., & Massey, D. (2020). Aligning the science of reading with adaptive teaching. *Reading Research Quarterly, 55*, S299–S306.

Woulfin, S., & Gabriel, R. E. (2020). Interconnected infrastructure for improving reading instruction. *Reading Research Quarterly, 55*, S109–S117.

Semantics is the study of context-independent meaning (Birner, 2018). It is at the center of the linguistic system as it governs the *literal* meaning or content of words, phrases, sentences, and text (Owens, 2016) and how they are combined (Kearns, 2011). *Encoding* semantics helps us express our thoughts and ideas while **decoding** allows us to understand one another. It is at this junction where we find meaning through signs and *symbols*, or as defined in *semiotics*, signs and their objects.

The discourse surrounding semantics has origins in multiple disciplines: psychology, logic and philosophy, anthropology, and of course, linguistics (Partee, 1995). Each field also has various approaches. Their differences, however, depend on (a) where emphasis is placed (e.g., structure; systems and models; concept discriminations, acquisition, and principles; or meaning in its essence) and (b) the respective research methodology (Partee, 1995).

In terms of linguistics, *formal semantics* employs logical and philosophical aspects such as compositionality which address how the meaning of words builds and integrates to make sentences in accordance with *syntactical structure* (Birner, 2018). *Lexical semantics* is concerned with the relationships between words and their meanings (e.g., synonyms, antonyms, homophones, homonyms, hyponyms, converseness, polysemy, and part/whole) (Wright, 2015) while *conceptual semantics* surrounds the cognitive structure of meaning in its most basic form (e.g., denotation) before layers of **context** are added (e.g., connotation).

Although reciprocal in nature and sometimes difficult to separate in application, a conceptual line is often drawn between semantics and **pragmatics** (Goddard, 1998; Saeed, 2016). Semantics and pragmatics are different, as pragmatics is concerned with how language is used, its overall intent, and how it changes with each social setting and situation. [Contributed by Rebecca Carpenter de Cortina]

Birner, B. (2018). *Language and meaning.* Routledge.

Goddard, C. (1998). *Semantic analysis: A practical introduction.* Oxford University Press.

Kearns, K. (2011). *Semantics* (2nd ed.). Palgrave Macmillan.

Owens, R. (2016). *Language development: An introduction* (9th ed.). Pearson.

Partee, B. H. (1995). Lexical semantics and compositionality. In D. N. Osherson, L. R. Gleitman, & M. Liberman (Eds.), *An invitation to cognitive science, Language* (2nd ed., Vol. 1, pp. 311–360). MIT Press.

Saeed, J. (2016). *Semantics* (4th ed.). Wiley-Blackwell.

Wright, W. E. (2015). *Foundations for teaching English language learners: Research, theory, policy, and practice* (2nd ed.). Caslon.

Sentence frames, also called *sentence templates* or *sentence stems*, offer students *scaffolding* for making meaning through writing or **discussion.** Sentence frames foster academic ***vocabulary,*** composition skills, reading **comprehension,** and deeper thinking (Snow & Katz, 2010).

By having sentence frames available, instructors immerse students in the *rhetorical moves* of a discipline by highlighting the dialogic nature of reading and writing (Graff & Birkenstein, 2014). Methods such as building sentence frame walls initiate students into the *disciplinary discourse* (Carrier & Tatum, 2006). Sentence frames also provide support for *Emergent bilinguals* (EBs) by combining language and content development. Sentence frames that adjust to students' language level offer EBs a means to partake in *content knowledge* more effectively through writing practice (Donnelly & Roe, 2010) and discussion.

Sentence frames can vary from fill-in-the-blank sentences with a word bank to a cloze procedure (Taylor, 1953) to more complex sentence templates (Graff & Birkenstein, 2014) that mirror the moves and organization that experienced disciplinary professionals make. For example, sentence frames can generate meaning making when students complete *I see..., I think..., I wonder...* statements or when they consider ***multiple perspectives,*** such as "Though I concede that _____, I still insist that_____" (Graff & Birkenstein, 2014, p. 298).

However, while sentence frames can offer a model for structure and organization, a teacher must explain the rhetorical moves of the frames so that students can reshape and adjust the sentences to suit their particular *purposes* (Graff & Birkenstein, 2014). Moreover, some students may feel the frames stifle their creativity and ideas, especially after the sentence frames' rhetorical moves are internalized. Therefore, sentence frames should act as optional ***scaffolds*** for students. [Contributed by Holly Sheppard Riesco]

Carrier, K. A., & Tatum, A. W. (2006). Creating sentence walls to help English-language learners develop content literacy. *The Reading Teacher, 60*(3), 285–288.

Donnelly, W. B., & Roe, C. J. (2010). Using sentence frames to develop academic vocabulary for English learners. *The Reading Teacher, 64*(2), 131–136.

Graff, G., & Birkenstein, C. (2014). *"They say/I say": The moves that matter in academic writing.* Third edition. New York: W.W. Norton & Company.

Snow, M. A., & Katz, A. (2010). English language development: Foundations and implementation in kindergarten through grade five. California Department of Education. In *Improving education for English learners: Research-based approaches* (pp. 83–148).

Taylor, W. L. (1953). "Cloze procedure": A new tool for measuring readability. *Journalism Quarterly, 30*(4), 415–433.

Shared reading/writing is a *collaborative* instructional approach in which teachers and students read and/or write together, steered by the instructional objective of providing support while slowly *releasing the responsibility* of **independent reading and writing** to students. During a large group, or in smaller groups implementing **guided reading**, students join the teacher or "share" the reading of a book chosen from a wide variety of **genres.** In early grades, the teacher may use an oversized big book or text projected on a screen and explicitly models *print concepts*, **fluency**, and **decoding.** The teacher *thinks aloud* about interactions with the text and *concept of print* while students read both pictures and text and make predictions, analyze the main idea, or discuss the author's purpose (Fountas & Pinnell, 1996). For example, the teacher might say, "I am noticing a word I do not know. What should I do?" In middle and upper grades, shared reading is a time when teachers and students read the same text together for specific instructional goals such as **scaffolding** deeper text engagement or text analysis using **critical literacy theory** (Allen, 2002).

In shared writing, the teacher and students write collaboratively, contributing to a single composition such as an original **narrative,** a report, a summary, or a letter. Shared writing can occur either in a large group or in smaller groups during **guided writing.** The teacher speaks aloud, explicitly **modeling** the *metacognition* involved in the **writing process.** Students contribute thoughts and ideas as the teacher acts as scribe and models the development of writing, **mechanics,** word choice and conventions. The teacher creates a safe place for students to talk about ideas, topics, and details to include in the piece. Generally, in this reciprocal version of writing, the teacher will model rereading and revision as the students are scaffolded to find confusing passages that need clarification and areas that need more detail or contain errors in punctuation, capitalization, or spelling. As an alternative, students may assume stratified roles in which the authors agree on the topic and pre-plan together, but each student individually drafts a section. This stratified approach is especially effective for digital writing which provides an option for real time collaborative editing. Some pieces will be short and completed in one session, and others will continue for several days or more and may be part of a **writers' workshop.** [Contributed by Leah R. Cheek] [See also Guided Reading/Writing; Independent Reading/Writing]

Allen, J. (2002). *On the same page: Shared reading beyond the primary grades.* Stenhouse.

Calkins, L. (2003). *Units of study for primary writing: A yearlong curriculum.* Heinemann.

Fountas, C., & Pinnell G. (1996). *Guiding reading, good first teaching for all children.* Heinemann.

McCarrier, A., Pinnell, G., & Fountas, C. (2000). *Interactive writing: How language & literacy come together, K-2.* Heinemann.

Sight words are words that a proficient reader has previously read, has retained in memory, and is able to retrieve quickly and effortlessly by sight. If a sight word is known well, the reader will activate the spelling, pronunciation, and meaning *fluently* without analysis or **decoding**, which allows the reader's focus to be on comprehending the text (Ehri & McCormick, 1998).

Sight words and high frequency words are often used as identical terms, although there is a distinction. *High frequency words* are those words which have been curated because of their common usage. High frequency words are often grouped into lists, such as the Fry, Dolch, or curriculum/program specific lists. Sight words are unique to each reader and can include high frequency words. This expanding, personal sight word list includes all the words the reader knows instantly and *automatically* (Miles, 2018). An ardent young paleontologist might know the word "Plateosaurus" by sight; a person with other interests might not.

Sight words can be added to a reader's personal sight word list both explicitly and implicitly. *Grapheme-phoneme* (letter-sound) connections can be explicitly taught and used to decode regularly-spelled words (Ehri, 2020). Words are stored in memory more efficiently using grapheme-phoneme connections as opposed to repetition and whole-word visual storage (Joshi et al., 2008). The process of pronouncing a printed word and storing the orthographic, or spelling, information is called *orthographic mapping*. This orthographic information can also be stored implicitly through self-teaching when a reader independently reads words (Share, 2008). The grapheme-phoneme connections made explicitly or implicitly are retained in memory and enable the reader to recognize words automatically by sight.

Sight word reading is an important *foundational reading skill* because it is the most efficient way of reading words, as opposed to decoding, analogizing, or predicting (Ehri, 2020). [Contributed by Wyann Stanton] [See also Decoding]

Ehri, L. S. (2020). The science of learning to read words: A case for systematic phonics instruction. *Reading Research Quarterly, 55*, S45–S60.

Ehri, L. C., & McCormick, S. (1998). Phases of word learning: Implications for instruction with delayed and disabled readers. *Reading & Writing Quarterly, 14*(2), 135–163.

Joshi, R. M., Treiman, R., Carreker, S., & Moats, L. C. (2008). How words cast their spell. *American Educator, 32*(4), 6–16.

Miles, K. P., Rubin, G. B., & Gonzalez-Frey, S. (2018). Rethinking sight words. *Reading Teacher, 71*(6), 715–726.

Share, D. L. (2008). Orthographic learning, phonological recoding, and self-teaching. *Advances in Child Development and Behavior, 36*, 31–82.

Simple View of Reading (SVR) (Gough & Tunmer, 1986) describes *literacy* acquisition using an equation: *decoding* (DC) multiplied by listening comprehension (LC) equals reading *comprehension* (RC) or DC × LC = RC. Although many have extended or objected to this simple view (see, for example, Carroll, 1993; Compton-Lilly et al., 2020; Francis et al., 2018; Snow, 2018), this equation does have explanatory and predictive power.

Reading *comprehension* is related to a reader's ability to understand *oral language*. **Background knowledge, vocabulary,** and knowledge of language structures are important to **understanding** a spoken message, and they also play a role in understanding written text. Reading comprehension is also dependent on *decoding* skills. When an unknown word appears in print, comprehension is possible only if a reader can determine what the word is. However, experienced readers recognize most words by sight, which also supports comprehension.

Scholars have decomposed the SVR to demonstrate components involved in decoding and listening comprehension. For example, Scarborough's rope (2001) depicts language comprehension and decoding as many-threaded strands, including background knowledge, verbal reasoning, **phonological awareness,** and more. These elaborated models acknowledge the complexity of the reading process but offer little about how readers integrate all of these processes and may lead to a compartmentalized, subskills approach to reading instruction (Compton-Lilly et al., 2020). Additionally, aspects such as working memory, **fluency,** *morphological analysis, metacognition, context,* **motivation** and the developmental processes of learning to read are not included. These aspects go beyond what occurs as a function of listening comprehension and decoding. [Contributed by Vicki Stewart Collet]

Carroll, J. B. (1993). *Human cognitive abilities: A survey of factor-analytic studies.* Cambridge University Press.

Compton-Lilly, C. F., Mitra, A., Guay, M., & Spence, L. K. (2020). A confluence of complexity: Intersections among reading theory, neuroscience, and observations of young readers. *Reading Research Quarterly, 55,* S185–S195.

Francis, D. J., Kulesz, P. A., & Benoit, J. S. (2018). Extending the simple view of reading to account for variation within readers and across texts: The Complete View of Reading (CVR i). *Remedial and Special Education, 39*(5), 274–288.

Gough, P. B., & Tunmer, W. E. (1986). Decoding, reading, and reading disability. *Remedial and Special Education, 7*(1), 6–10.

Scarborough, H. S. (2001). Connecting early language and literacy to later reading (dis)abilities: Evidence, theory, and practice. In S. Neuman & D. Dickinson (Eds.), *Handbook for research in early literacy* (pp. 97–110). Guilford Press.

Snow, C. E. (2018). Simple and not-so-simple views of reading. *Remedial and Special Education, 39*(5), 313–316.

Small-group instruction in contemporary classrooms is a useful and pervasive instructional practice that promotes enhanced learning, social *engagement*, and accountability through flexible, homogeneous or heterogeneous grouping of two or more students (Murphy, 2017).

Flexible grouping allows teachers to create and change groupings based on students' interests, levels, and needs identified through observation or ***assessment***, as opposed to *fixed grouping*, which creates year-long static groups without fluidity (Bates, 2013).

Homogeneous grouping is placing students together by similar level or similar need, which allows teachers to provide *differentiated*, personalized instruction. Two examples of homogeneous grouping are ***guided reading***, which uses grouping by similar reading levels, and ***intervention***, which uses grouping by similar assessed need.

Heterogeneous grouping is putting students together by different levels or abilities, allowing teachers to utilize student *diversity* for *peer collaboration*, interdependence, and enhanced student learning (Murphy, 2017). Two examples of heterogeneous grouping are cooperative learning groups and text-based ***discussion*** groups.

Immediate and individualized *feedback*, including error correction, is an important benefit of small-group instruction and can be provided by teachers or by peers within the group. By correcting errors when they are first made, errors will most likely not become internalized and repeated (Gersten, 2014).

By combining research evidence on effective classroom instruction with effective small-group instruction that is explicit, comprehensive, intensive, and supportive, the ***literacy*** needs of students can be met, including those who are most at risk of failure (Foorman, 2001). [Contributed by Wyann Stanton] [See also Intervention]

Bates, C. C. (2013). Flexible grouping during literacy centers: A model for differentiating instruction. *YC Young Children, 68*(2), 30.

Foorman, B. R., & Torgesen, J. (2001). Critical elements of classroom and small-group instruction promote reading success in all children. *Learning Disabilities Research & Practice: A Publication of the Division for Learning Disabilities, Council for Exceptional Children, 16*(4), 203–212.

Gersten, R., Compton, D., Connor, C. M., Dimino, J., Santoro, L., Linan-Thompson, S., & David Tilly, W. (2014). Assisting students struggling with reading: Response to intervention and multi-tier intervention in the primary grades. *Improving Outcomes for Students with or at Risk for Reading Disabilities*, 121–190.

Murphy, P. K., Greene, J. A., Firetto, C. M., Li, M., Lobczowski, N. G., Duke, R. F., Wei, L., & Croninger, R. M. V. (2017). Exploring the influence of homogeneous versus heterogeneous grouping on students' text-based discussions and comprehension. *Contemporary Educational Psychology, 51*, 336–355.

Sociocultural perspectives emphasize the role of social interaction and cultural and historical influences in learning and the contextual situatedness of *literacy* practices. Central to this work have been the theories of *Vygotsky* (1978), which posit that cognitive changes have their genesis in social interaction. Learning is not simply an acquisition of knowledge, but a process of social participation. Social learning precedes, and leads to, development. Cognitive functions, even those carried out alone, are affected by the values and intellectual tools of the cultural context.

Sociocultural theories view language as a product of the social environment, a tool for communication that has a powerful role in shaping thought. Vygotsky (1978) hypothesized that language learning moves from the *interpsychological* (social) plane to the *intrapsychological* (internal) one through interaction and *imitation*. However, imitation, in Vygotsky's view, view "is not simply a reproduction of what he has experienced, but a creative reworking of the impressions he has acquired. He combines them and uses them to construct a new reality, one that conforms to his own needs and desires" (Vygotsky 2004, p. 11).

Sociocultural theorists consider texts in relation to social purposes. Construction of meaning is viewed as a shared enterprise, and instruction as contingent and situated. Children bring a range of cultural knowledge, experiences, and skills to school literacy tasks, which could be recognized and utilized during literacy instruction (Gonzalez et al., 2004). Emphasis is placed on the use of mental and material tools to mediate learning processes. Sociocultural views vary on the role assumed by teachers: as a *more knowledgeable other* (Vygotsky, 1978) or as a co-participator and *collaborator* (Gutiérrez et al., 1997). [Contributed by Vicki Stewart Collet] [See also Culturally Responsive Instruction; Zone of Proximal Development]

Gonzalez, N., Moll, L. C., & Amanti, C. (2004). *Funds of knowledge: Theorizing practices in households, communities, and classrooms.* Lawrence Erlbaum Associates.

Gutiérrez, K., Baquedano-Lopez, P., & Turner, M. (1997). Putting language back into language arts: When the radical middle meets the third space. *Language Arts, 74*(5), 368–378.

Vygotsky, L. S. (1978). *Mind in society: The development of higher psychological processes.* Harvard University Press.

Vygotsky, L. S. (2004). Imagination and creativity in childhood. *Journal of Russian and East European Psychology, 42*(1), 7–97.

Standards, or *academic standards,* describe what students should know, understand, and be able to do. Standards may describe learning benchmarks at the end of a unit, course, or program, or at grade- or age-levels. Thus, *literacy* standards describe a developmental continuum of reading, writing, listening, and speaking. For example, a first-grade standard might require students to *retell* stories and understand their key messages; standards may expect students graduating from high school to be able to write in different formats (reports, essays, literary criticism, etc.) to demonstrate proficiency. A goal of academic standards is to ensure all students are taught the same core skills.

Standards describe a destination but do not prescribe how to get there. They are the "what" of education, while *curriculum* is the "how." Standards are intended to guide decision-making regarding the teaching materials and methods selected for the curriculum (the plan for instruction). Standards may also guide the development of **assessments.** For example, in *standardized testing,* students are given the same test to identify whether individuals, and schools or systems, are meeting the standards.

Although many countries have national standards, in the U.S., states or local communities have the purview to set academic standards. However, a shift occurred with the creation of the *Common Core State Standards* (ccss) by working groups from the National Governors Association Center for Best Practices and the Council of Chief State School Officers (2010). Local entities initially felt pressures to adopt these literacy and math standards when the U.S. Department of Education announced that eligibility for federal grant funding was restricted to states adopting such standards (Collet et al., 2020). Initially, these pressures resulted in adoption of ccss by 45 states; however, the number of implementers declined as states withdrew from adoption of the standards, mostly because of bi-partisan political backlash (Camera, 2015). Standards subsequently adopted by many states bore strong resemblance to ccss, however, moving the U.S. toward national standards and testing, a practice that has been commonplace in many countries for decades. [Contributed by Vicki Stewart Collet]

Camera, L. (2015, September 21). *As test results trickle in, states still ditching Common Core.* U.S. News and World Report.

Collet, V. S., Endacott, J. L., Goering, C. Z., Denny, G., Jennings, J. A., & Norton, G. P. (2020). Leadership hybridity: Examining teachers' perceptions of standards-based reform. *Journal of School Leadership, 30*(5), 444–464.

National Governors Association Center for Best Practices & The Council of Chief State School Officers. (2010). *Common Core State Standards for English Language Arts.* http://www.corestandards.org/assets/CCSSI_ELA%20Standards.pdf

Story elements/story grammar are interchangeable terms describing features that contribute to the overall structure and meaning in fictional literature. Just as *grammar* rules are used to structure sentences, story grammar provides a structure for a *narrative text*. In the simplest form, story elements or story grammar include the setting, characters, and plot. The *setting* is the physical location of the action in the story, or where and when the story takes place. In narratives, the *characters* are usually people or animals. Authors typically use characters' dialogue and actions to move the story along or to advance the plot. *Plot* relates to the events that happen in the story and typically begins with a problem and ends with the resolution of the problem.

As students become proficient at identifying the setting, characters and plot, additional complex story elements are introduced. These include conflict, theme, point of view and tone. The *conflict* is the problem or challenge in the plot that is the focus of the story. Students can learn to identify the conflict, the response to the conflict, the action the characters take after identifying the conflict, and the eventual outcome. *Theme* is described as the underlying moral or idea the author is expressing throughout the story. Sometimes this is referred to as the author's message. A teacher might ask the students, "Why did the author write this story?" Next, when students identify the *point of view*, they analyze to discover who is telling the story and what is their *perspective.* Sometimes the point of view is from the perspective of one of the characters, and sometimes it is from the perspective of the unseen narrator. Finally, the *tone* is the attitude the author conveys toward the subjects and theme. The tone can also evoke a mood or connection in the reader.

Although ***understanding*** how a story is organized provides a pathway for students to increase reading connections, predictions, and ***comprehension*** (Dymock, 2007), story grammar should not be viewed as the isolated and correct approach to narrative writing, ignoring other innovative approaches. Through the *reading-writing relationship*, the ability to identify and analyze story grammar transfers to students' own writing and can act as a guide as writers practice and implement organizing their thoughts to tell a story. [Contributed by Leah R. Cheek] [See also Narrative Text]

Dymock, S. (2007). Comprehension strategy instruction: Teaching narrative text structure awareness. *The Reading Teacher, 61*(2), 161–167.

Rumelhart, D. (1975). Notes on schema for stories. In D. Bobrow & A. Collins (Eds.), *Representation and understanding: Studies in cognitive science.* Academic.

Young, T., Bryan, G., Jacobs, J., & Tunnell. (2020). *Children's literature, briefly.* Pearson.

Text structure is the way in which the author has situated the information for the reader. The text structure acts as a map or guide giving clues to the reader to follow as they read the text. *Informational text* has five primary structures: 1) cause and effect, 2) chronological/sequence, 3) compare and contrast, 4) description or list, and 5) problem and solution (Moss, 2004), which may occur in combination within a text. *Cause and effect* structure is when something that has happened is described along with the effect it had. *Chronological* or *sequence text* is presented in historical or procedural order. *Compare* and *contrast* is used to describe how two or more things are similar or how they are different. A *description* or *list structure* details a thing or idea. Finally, *problem and solution* is structured to present a problem and then an author posits a way or ways to solve it. Literary text usually follows a story structure, sometimes referred to as ***story grammar***, with *plot*, *setting*, and *characters*.

Text features support a reader's ***comprehension*** of a text, influence ***vocabulary*** development, and are an integral part of text structures (Herman et al., 1987). There are four main categories of features: print, illustrations, organizational aids, and graphic aids. Examples of these include: a table of contents, pictures, bolded headings, and tables or charts. These are often an engaging, entertaining way to emphasize the content.

Educators could teach text structures and features to help readers know what to expect and to help them determine what is important in the text. *Signal words* could be taught to students to support their ***understanding*** of the text structure. These signal words are ***genre*** and structure type indicators that guide the reader (Williams, 2007). For example, a signal word could be "first," or "one reason." Knowing the text structure can also help the reader *summarize* the text and contributes to their overall comprehension. "Students who learn to use the organization and structure of ***informational texts*** are better able to comprehend and retain the information found in them" (Moss, 2004, p. 711). [Contributed by Afton Schleiff] [See also Story Elements/Story Grammar; Informational Text]

Herman, P., Anderson, R., Pearson, P., & Nagy, W. (1987). Incidental acquisition of word meaning from expositions with varied text features. *Reading Research Quarterly, 22*(3), 263–284.

Moss, B. (2004). Teaching expository text structures through information trade book retellings. *The Reading Teacher, 57*(8), 710–718.

Williams, J. P. (2007). Literacy in the curriculum: Integrating text structure and content area instruction. In D. S. McNamara (Ed.), *Reading comprehension strategies: Theories, interventions, and technologies* (pp. 199–220). Lawrence Erlbaum Associates Publishers.

Theme is a central meaning, message, or idea that runs throughout a story and contains an author's thoughts about humanity. Theme has also been defined as "a relationship among story components in a form that is abstracted from the specific story context, and it comments on that relationship in some way" (Williams et al., 2002, p. 236). Sometimes in younger elementary grades, theme is defined or explained as the lesson or moral of the story (Morgan et al., 2021). Themes tend to be revealed over the course of a text and are not explicitly stated (Au, 1992). Readers can draw on *characters, plot, setting,* and *dialogue* to construct themes. Themes are sometimes written as one word, but, more appropriately, are a complete sentence that expresses a deeper ***understanding*** of the text. Oftentimes texts contain more than one theme.

Students as young as kindergarten have demonstrated the ability to group texts with similar themes together, while students in the fourth grade have a more nuanced understanding (Lehr, 1988). Thematic analysis can serve to foster intertextual and intercontextual links to texts illustrating a similar thematic focus. Lehr (1988) also discovered that because themes are abstract, students may struggle and remain at the concrete level when creating themes. Exposing students to a variety of literature contributes to their theme ***comprehension*** (Au, 1992). ***Background knowledge*** and life experience play an important role in students developing an understanding of theme, and because of this, the skill of formulating theme is refined as readers grow.

Readers construct themes, they don't identify them (Morgan et al., 2021). When co-constructing with partners or small groups, students' ability to create themes was enhanced through ***discussion*** (Au, 1992). "Ultimately, teaching for theme is helping students develop a process of noticing and gathering, for the purpose of learning from and taking the themes they have constructed into the real world even as they leave the story world behind" (Morgan et al., 2021, p. 437). [Contributed by Afton Schleiff] [See also Background Knowledge]

Au, K. H. (1992). Constructing the theme of a story. *Language Arts, 69*(2), 106–111.

Lehr, S. (1988). The child's developing sense of theme as a response to literature. *Reading Research Quarterly, 23*(3), 337–357.

Morgan, D. N., Evans, K. I., Defrancesco, J. (2021). "Theme doesn't just jump out": Teaching for theme comprehension. *The Reading Teacher, 74*(4), 429–438.

Williams, J. P., Lauer, K. D., Hall, K. M., Lord, K. M., Gugga, S. S., Bak, S.-J., Jacobs, P. R., & deCani, J. S. (2002). Teaching elementary school students to identify story themes. *Journal of Educational Psychology, 94*(2), 235–248.

A **thesis**, often in the form of a *thesis statement,* is a writer's controlling idea or *claim* in a non-literary work. Unlike a descriptive or factual statement that simply articulates an inarguable observation or truth, a thesis is a debatable or possibly controversial statement in which the writer must prove the veracity of their stance with relevant, sufficient *evidence* and a logical line of reasoning. Additionally, an effective, defensible thesis asserts a clear and specific claim, usually acknowledging the complexity of the position; an ineffective thesis may be too vague, narrow, or obvious. By positioning an effective thesis near the introduction of an essay, it "enables the reader to enter the essay with a clear sense that its writer has something to prove...and shapes their expectations" (Mays, 2017, p. 1893).

According to Shea, Scanlon, and Aufses (2013), there are several types of thesis statements that writers can employ: a closed thesis, an open thesis, or a thesis acknowledging a counterargument. In a closed thesis statement, the writer explicitly delineates the main points of the argument, usually articulating two or three points. While an open thesis statement does express the overall point of the writing, it does not list the specific subpoints the writer intends to discuss because they may be extensive. A writer may also address the counterargument in their thesis to establish their argument as a reasonable or complex claim (pp. 95–96).

Ultimately, it is a writer's ability to support a thesis with convincing evidence and reasoning throughout the work that determines if the thesis is strong or weak (Prendergast, 2015, p. 60). Because of this, writers may begin the ***writing process*** with a working thesis—a position that is not yet fully-formed—that evolves into a more nuanced, focused, and well-supported thesis as the writer discovers more about their topic through research and testing the validity and reliability of the thesis through dialogue with others. This is the opposite of "thesis-first writing" in which a writer's thesis remains static despite new discoveries or changing positions during the writing process; this could lead to uninspired and disengaged writing (Duxbury, 2008). Instead, writers should embrace revision when crafting a thesis to accurately reflect the evidence and thinking uncovered in the recursive writing process. [Contributed by Kathryn Hackett-Hill] [See also Argumentative Writing]

Duxbury, A. (2008). The tyranny of the thesis statement. *English Journal, 97*(4), 16–18.

Mays, K. J. (2017). *The Norton introduction to literature* (12th ed.). W.W. Norton & Company.

Prendergast, C. (2015). *Can I use I? Because I hate, hate, hate college writing* (H. Lindahl, Illus.). Out of Pocket Press.

Shea, R. H., Scanlon, L., & Aufses, R. D. (2013). *The language of composition: Reading, writing, rhetoric* (2nd ed.). Bedford/St. Martin's.

Think aloud is the act of a teacher or student *modeling* their thought processes verbally. Typically, a think aloud serves as a metacognitive model when processing a topic or text. Modeling *metacognition* is important because it can be used to regulate reading processes that build *comprehension.* In the 1950s, think aloud developed as a "tool of inquiry into cognitive processing" (Kucan & Beck, 1997, p. 273).

Thinking aloud can be a method of instruction whereby the teacher illuminates what readers do during reading. Educators may model reading strategies, metacognition, affective reactions, and reflection through verbally processing their thoughts. Studies reviewed by Kucan and Beck (1997) demonstrated that a teacher-led think aloud enhanced comprehension and student performance on *assessments.* Pressley et al. (1992) categorized think aloud as a transactional strategy because teachers and students work together to create meaning.

When a teacher is listening to a student thinking aloud, she can "gain insights about meaning construction and comprehension difficulties" (Pressley et al., 1992, pp. 538–539). However, the think aloud strategy may not benefit all students. One study found that beginning English language learners did not find success through this strategy like their intermediate counterparts (McKeown & Gentilucci, 2011).

Using think alouds, Lau et al. (2006) found "good readers tended to use more reading strategies than did poor readers during their reading process" (p. 389). Think alouds can also be used to assess student writing: students verbalize their thinking as they write while the teacher notices where obstacles are encountered, observes students' strengths, and notes the student's *writing process* (Beck, 2018). Self-regulatory skills also become apparent during a think aloud when a student self-adjusts their behavior and mental processes to meet the task at hand. [Contributed by Afton Schleiff]

Beck, S. (2018). *A think-aloud approach to writing assessment: Analyzing process and product with adolescent writers.* Teachers College Press.

Kucan, L., & Beck, I. (1997). Thinking aloud and reading comprehension research: Inquiry, instruction, and social interaction. *Review of Educational Research, 67*(3), 271–299.

Lau, K. (2006). Reading strategy use between chinese good and poor readers: A think-aloud study. *Journal of Research in Reading, 29*(4), 383–399.

McKeown, R. G., & Gentilucci, J. L. (2007). Think aloud strategy: Metacognitive development and monitoring comprehension in the middle school second-language classroom. *Journal of Adolescent & Adult Literacy, 51*(2), 136–147.

Pressley, M., Beard El Dinary, P., Gaskins, I., Schuder, T., Bergman, J. L., Almasi, J., & Brown, R. (1992). Beyond direct explanation: Transactional instruction of reading comprehension strategies. *The Elementary School Journal, 92*(5), 513–555.

Transactional theory, also known as *Reader Response theory,* describes an active process of meaning making between a reader and the text. As proposed in this theory, meaning is considered as not inside the text or inside the reader, but instead, happens between the two (Rosenblatt, 1994). The text helps to focus what the reader pays attention to and readers activate *prior knowledge* and experience during the transaction (Rosenblatt, 1978).

In Transactional theory, there are two different *stances* that readers take when reading: *efferent* and *aesthetic*. These stances are represented on a continuum with the scope of attention shifting from the public to private sphere. Readers take an efferent stance when they focus their attention outward in order to obtain information and then perform an action or retain information (Rosenblatt, 1994). When readers take an aesthetic stance, they attend to their own feelings, senses, and ideas and to the images and concepts in the text. The reader's attention in the aesthetic stance is on the reader's lived-through experiences and is a process of evoking and responding (Rosenblatt, 1978). "Rosenblatt maintains that aesthetic response is primary in the reader's personal transaction with a text, and at the same time urges readers to examine personal factors that enter into their response, potentially allowing them to change and grow into mature readers" (Cai, 2008, p. 219). Efferent and aesthetic stances do not refer to the type of text, but rather the reader's stance when reading the text. For example, a literary text could be read from either stance.

Transactional theory and efferent and aesthetic stances describe opportunities for readers to approach a text with different *purposes* and to interact differently with texts. In doing so, it describes the opportunity for readers to selectively focus their attention on extracting information or considering their own thoughts, feelings, and experiences. Students studying ***multicultural literature*** could incorporate a *critical **perspective*** that fosters reflection and transformation in order to enhance their efferent and aesthetic responses (Cai, 2008). [Contributed by Afton Schleiff]

Cai, M. (2008). Transactional theory and the study of multicultural literature. *Language Arts,* *85*(3), 212–220.

Rosenblatt, L. M. (1978). *The reader, the text, the poem: The transactional theory of the literary work.* Southern Illinois University Press.

Rosenblatt, L. M. (1994). The transactional theory of reading and writing. In R. B. Ruddell, M. R. Ruddell, & H. Singer (Eds.), *Theoretical models and processes of reading* (pp. 1057–1092). International Reading Association.

Translanguaging is the interactive process multilingual speakers use to access their entire linguistic repertoire to make meaning and share their thoughts and ideas with others. It is also described as unitary in that a speaker's language practices are not viewed as separate, but rather an intertwined system that is dynamic, flexible, and transformative (García & Li Wei, 2014; Wright, 2015). Translanguaging reflects current languaging theories of how social action and self-reflection can inform and create supportive relationships and learning environments (Beach &Beauchemin, 2019).

In applying an *assets-based **perspective***, translanguaging classrooms (a) draw on co-existing language practices and cultural ***understandings*** that derive, build upon, and are enriched by three spheres—home, school, and community; (b) believe parents, families, and communities provide valuable *funds of knowledge* and must be included in the learning process; and (c) position the classroom as a *community of learners* where students and teachers co-create knowledge, challenge the status quo, and advocate for *equity* and equality (García et al., 2016).

A teacher who embraces translanguaging pedagogy will take on three strands: (1) *stance*, believe students have one repertoire which draws on all of their language features; (2) *design*, plan and create learning environments that engage students as active learners and welcome all language resources; and (3) *shift*, embrace flexibility and fluidity, adjusting and responding to circumstances of the moment so students are free to think, speak, and learn (García et al., 2016).

In sum, whether translanguaging is described as above or as going between and beyond different linguistic structures and systems (Li Wei, 2011), or the shuttling between languages of an integrated system to co-construct meaning (Canagarajah, 2011), it underscores the importance of social interaction and returns power to the speaker through agency and choice. [Contributed by Rebecca Carpenter de Cortina]

Beach, R., & Beauchemin, F. (2019). *Teaching language as action in the ELA classroom*. Routledge.

Canagarajah, S. (2011). Codemeshing in academic writing: Identifying teachable strategies of translanguaging. *The Modern Language Journal, 95*, 401–417.

García, O., Ibarra Johnson, S., & Seltzer, K. (2016). *The translanguaging classroom: Leveraging student bilingualism for learning*. Caslon.

García, O., & Li Wei. (2014). *Translanguaging: Languaging, bilingualism and education*. Palgrave Macmillian.

Li Wei. (2011). Moment analysis and translanguaging space: Discursive construction of identities by multilingual Chinese youth in Britain. *Journal of Pragmatics, 43*(5), 1222–1235.

Wright, W. E. (2015). *Foundations for teaching English language learners: Research, theory, policy, and practice* (2nd ed.). Caslon.

Understanding is the ability to think about and use concepts, to explain, interpret, and apply knowledge. Understanding is grasping the full meaning of something.

Understanding is built, not acquired; worked for, not supplied. It is not heard or read but considered and deduced. Reading alone does not create understanding, although pondering what was read could lead to it. When you understand, you extend the information given and make meaning of your own. Understanding is insightful, nuanced, coherent, and thorough. When you understand, you can substantiate or justify. You don't borrow an expert opinion, you internalize an idea. Understanding can't be given to someone; they have to work for it themselves. "The tuition of effort and diligence must be paid to own understanding" (Collet, 2019, p. 90).

Understanding is built on knowledge—both *content knowledge* and *procedural knowledge* of how things are done. These forms of knowledge are building blocks for understanding. To understand, you must know, but you must do something with what you know to generate understanding. Understanding is conceptual. It is made up of conclusions that are derived or grasped, not simply told or memorized (Wiggins & McTighe, 2005). Understanding is deep. It includes *inferences* and insights, principles and generalizations that go beyond the obvious.

If understanding is a goal, learners must be meaning-makers, not meaning-takers. Understanding is more-likely to be generated when learners are agentive in the learning process. When understanding is the goal, classroom *discussions* go beyond recitation. Recitation allows a person to convey his understanding, but doesn't allow him to develop it (Newkirk, 2017). When teachers target understanding, they aren't looking for set answers; classroom discussions encourage exploratory talk that engages students with formulating, refining, and extending an idea.

When we understand, we can adjust and apply our learning in varied and unique situations. In complex, real-world circumstances, answers do not come neatly packaged; knowledge and skills are insufficient. When confronted with new challenges and contexts, insight guides effective response. Understanding is built and evidenced in the doing. [Contributed by Vicki Stewart Collet]

Collet, V. S. (2019). *Collaborative lesson study*. Teachers College Press.

Newkirk, T. (2017). *Embarrassment: And the emotional underlife of learning*. Heinemann.

Wiggins, G. P., & McTighe, J. (2005). *The understanding by design guide to creating high-quality units*. ASCD.

Vocabulary instruction supports students in learning word meanings. There is not a one-size-fits-all strategy for teaching vocabulary; however, there are a plethora of pedagogically sound strategies that teachers can choose from (Ash &Baumann, 2017). Vocabulary can be separated into two primary categories: receptive and expressive. *Receptive vocabulary* includes words we understand when we hear and read them, while *expressive vocabulary* includes words we use in speech and writing. This difference is important when we consider that there are different levels of word knowledge. Words we encounter fall into one of four categories: unknown words, initial recognition (we have seen or heard but not sure of meaning/do not use in our speech), partial recognition (we know one meaning in print/could use it in a sentence), or full word knowledge (we know more than one meaning in print contexts/can use the word in various situations).

Words can be sorted into three tiers (Beck et al., 2002). *Tier one words* are common in speech and are rarely explicitly taught. *Tier two words* are *academic words* that have broad applications and are usually connected with a known concept that supports **understanding** through *contextual cues*. *Tier three words* are specialized words that are associated with specific subject areas or abstract concepts. Tier three words may require *explicit instruction* in order to achieve full word knowledge.

Children learn words by being immersed in language. *Indirect teaching methods* include **read alouds**, wide **independent reading**, and talk activities (Mol & Bus, 2011). These are effective for learning tier one and many tier two words. Explicit strategies for teaching tier two and three words are diverse. For example, strategies may focus on *word attack* (using **morphology** to break a word into meaningful parts), memory strategies (KIM strategy: Frayer model, key idea, information and a memory clue) or word associations (synonyms, antonyms, homophones and homographs). Key ideas that are found in vocabulary research are repeated exposure and use, learning words in context, and strategic word selection (Biemiller & Boote, 2006). [Contributed by Savanna L. Gragg]

Ash, G. E., & Baumann, J. F. (2017). Vocabulary and reading comprehension: The nexus of meaning. In *The handbook of research on reading comprehension* (2nd ed., pp. 377–405). The Guilford Press.

Beck, I., McKeown, M., & Kunan, L. (2002). *Bringing words to life: Robust vocabulary instruction.* IGuilford.

Biemiller, A., & Boote, C. (2006). An effective method for building meaning vocabulary in primary grades. *Journal of Educational Psychology, 98*(1), 44–62.

Mol, S. E., & Bus, A. (2011). To read or not to read: A meta-analysis of print exposure from infancy to early adulthood. *Psychological Bulletin, 137*(2), 267–296.

Voice in writing *genres* is difficult to define given its subjective nature, but most definitions consider an author's stylistic choices such as syntax, tone, diction, and ideological and ethical values (Phelan, 2014). *Style* and voice are frequently used interchangeably, although voice most often refers to the texture and sound of a text while style refers to tangible elements and *mechanics* of an author's writing (Elbow, 2007). The sociopolitical implications of voice can also affect the definition to varying degrees, given that some discourse communities privilege certain voices over others (Matsuda & Jeffery, 2012). For example, most *academic discourse* communities in the U.S. expect students to write using *Standard American English,* so writing voices become more homogenous and less varied.

Voice is often developed in light of a writer's *purpose* and *audience,* making voice a fluid concept. The options available for crafting voice for a specific audience and/or genre is what can make voice so difficult to define. Writers who work to create a specific voice must take into account audience and genre, and as is often the case for student writers, *assessment* criteria and *rubrics* (Matsuda & Jeffery, 2012) This attention to audience and purpose would align with a "rhetorical narrative view of communication" (Phelan, 2014). Within this view, writers create voice through the use of diction, *syntax,* and *tone* (Phelan, 2014). Christine Tardy classifies voice into three categories: the social, the individual, and the dialogic (Tardy, 2012). This approach to further defining voice acknowledges the roles *discourse communities,* personal preference, and ongoing conversations play in shaping a writer's voice. Writers may also use double-voicing, adopting or parodying other's language (Bakhtin, 1981).

Writing instructors who seek to examine voice alongside students must be aware of its varying definitions, interpretations, and executions. Rather than approaching voice as a fixed criterium, it is important to consider students' personal discourse communities and their familiarity with other discourse communities as well as any forms of assessment assigned to pieces of writing. [Contributed by Megan Yates Grizzle]

Bakhtin, M. (1981). *The dialogic imagination* (M. Holquist & C. Emerson, Trans. and Ed.). University of Austin Press.

Elbow, P. (2007). Voice in writing again: Embracing contraries. *College English, 70*(2), 168–188.

Matsuda P. K., & Jeffery, J. V. (2012). Voice in student essays. In K. Hyland & C. S. Guinda (Eds.), *Stance and voice in written academic genres.* Palgrave Macmillan.

Phelan, J. (2014). Voice, tone, and the rhetoric of narrative communication. *Language and Literature, 23*(1), 49–60.

Tardy, C. M. (2012). Current conceptions of voice. In K. Hyland & C. S. Guinda (Eds.), *Stance and voice in written academic genres.* Palgrave Macmillan.

Workshop (reading and writing) is an active approach to instruction which focuses on the learners as individuals. The workshop structure begins with a teacher-directed whole group *mini-lesson*, a brief time of *explicit instruction*, followed by goal-driven *independent* student interaction with text. Guided by the belief that frequent *feedback* through conferencing enables the creation of clear learning goals for reading and writing, the teacher *confers* with students one-on-one or in *small groups* during this independent work phase. The teacher communicates what she has noticed about the learner and provides suggestions for growth. Students communicate about their interaction with the written word and personally reflect on their learning. Midway through the workshop, the teacher generally pauses the independent work and quickly addresses an instructional point for additional *scaffolding*. Finally, the workshop session concludes with a whole group sharing time when the teacher and students communicate about their learning and reveal ideas about books or read aloud from their writing (Calkins, 2003).

The workshop model values ***mentor texts*** as quality literature and recognizes, "...students apply what they learn in reading to their own writing" (Fountas & Pinnell, 2001). Students read and write daily and are empowered to make their own choices about what they read and how to use writing as a tool for communication and reflection. The workshop model is designed to create an authentic, safe classroom culture in which students are empowered to use their own *voice* to tell their own individual stories through reading, writing, and speaking. [Contributed by Leah R. Cheek] [See also Independent Reading/Writing]

Calkins, L. (1986). *The art of teaching writing.* Heinemann.

Calkins, L. (2003). *Units of study for primary writing: A yearlong curriculum.* FirstHand.

Fountas, C., & Pinnell, G. (2001). *Guiding readers and writers. Teaching comprehension, genre, and content literacy.* Heinemann.

Graves, D. (1983). *Writing: Teachers and children at work.* Heinemann.

Writing process most commonly refers to the stages of writing an author moves through as he or she works toward a finished piece. The term "writing process" is not definable in any one concrete way but rather speaks to the idea that writing is an evolving and ever-changing act.

At its most basic, the writing process can be broken down into three categories: planning, sentence generation, and *revision* (Hayes & Flower, 1987). During the planning stage, writers generate basic ideas regarding structure and organization, *purpose*, and topic. Sentence generation refers to the physical and mental act of transmitting words to a page, and the revision stage is required to refine aspects of a written piece such as craft, *style*, organization, and *grammar*. While the stages of writing are fairly straightforward, the influences upon the process itself vary. Some scholars suggest that writers enter the writing process as a response to a specific rhetorical situation while others suggest that writers allow "syntactical and lexical choices to guide the process" (Flower & Hayes, 1981, p. 365).

Process Writing. Process writing is not to be confused with the writing process but is instead a strategy for engaging in the act of writing itself. Process writing provides writers with opportunities to complete more manageable writing tasks as they work through the phases of the writing process listed above. Writers might also feel less pressure as they work through process writing tasks because process writing tasks, such as pre-writing, group composition, or self-editing, are not intended to be assessed according to predetermined criteria. The act of *freewriting*, which asks writers to write without restrictions for a set amount of time, is an example of process writing. As Peter Elbow argues, "we have little hope of producing excellent writing unless we write a great deal" (Elbow, 1998, p. XIX). Process writing allows writers the opportunity to produce and examine pieces of writing without the pressure of final *assessment* and evaluation. [Contributed by Megan Yates Grizzle]

Elbow, P. (1998). *Writing with power: Techniques for mastering the writing process.* Oxford University Press.

Flower, L., & Hayes, J. (1981). A cognitive process theory of writing. *College Composition and Communication, 32*(4), 365–387.

Hayes, J. R., & Flower, L. S. (1987). On the structure of the writing process. *Topics in Language Disorders, 7*(4), 19–30.

Zone of Proximal Development (ZPD) is a term coined by *Vygotsky* (1978), which he defined as "the distance between the actual development level as determined by independent problem solving and the level of potential development as determined through problem solving under adult guidance or in *collaboration* with more capable *peers*" (p. 86). Put another way, "What the child is able to do in collaboration today he will be able to do independently tomorrow" (Vygotsky, 1987, p. 211).

Bodrova and Leong (2007) emphasize the significance of the word *zone*—Vygotsky viewed it not as some single point of development but as a continuum of progress—and of the word *proximal*—that ZPD refers to the learning and behaviors that are closest to emerging. As Chaiklin (2003) notes, ZPD is relative and ever-changing: as learners develop, their ZPD progresses, and individual children's zones of proximal development differ. Working within the ZPD, learners imitate the more capable peer or mentor—not as a perfunctory copying of behaviors but as evidence of emerging **understanding,** suggesting that learners in the ZPD have developed enough to understand how to use the guidance or demonstration of the more competent other, even if they cannot yet perform the behavior independently (Chaiklin, 2003).

Educators often take up the idea of ZPD as they plan instructional strategies for their classroom; for example, teachers might **read aloud** and have a student repeat their words, or they might write in front of their students before inviting them to create their own writing. Although these practices are examples of **scaffolding,** Smagorinsky (2018) warns that ZPD as Vygotsky conceived it is more *individualized* and culturally-situated, necessitating mutual understanding and negotiation between a teacher and an individual student, and that ZPD is more concerned with long-term human development than with individual classroom activities or skills. [Contributed by Johnny B. Allred]

Bodrova, E., & Leong, D. J. (2007). The Zone of Proximal Development. *Tools of the mind: The Vygotskian approach to early childhood education* (2nd ed., pp. 39–49). Pearson.

Chaiklin, S. (2003). The Zone of Proximal Development in Vygotsky's analysis of learning and instruction. In A. Kozulin, B. Gindis, V. S. Ageyev, & S. M. Miller (Eds.), *Vygotsky's educational theory in cultural context* (pp. 39–64). Cambridge University Press.

Smagorinsky, P. (2018). Deconflating the ZPD and instructional scaffolding: Retranslating and reconceiving the zone of proximal development as the zone of next development. *Learning, Culture, and Social Interaction, 16,* 70–75.

Vygotsky, L. S. (1978). *Mind in society: The development of higher psychological processes.* Harvard University Press.

Vygotsky, L. S. (1987). Thinking and speech. In R. Rieber & A. Carton (Eds.), *L.S. Vygotsky, collected works* (Vol. 1, pp. 39–285). Plenum.

Index

Printed in the United States
by Baker & Taylor Publisher Services